Lone Wolf Mentality

A Millennial Mindset

BENJAMIN PHILLIPS III

cover photo: Mircea Costina/Shutterstock.com

Printed in the United States of America
Published by Braughler Books LLC., Springboro, Ohio

First printing, 2019

ISBN: 978-1-970063-09-7 soft cover
ISBN: 978-1-970063-10-3 ebook

Library of Congress Control Number: 2019902877

Ordering information: Special discounts are available on quantity purchases by bookstores, corporations, associations, and others. For details, contact the publisher at:

sales@braughlerbooks.com

or at 937-58-BOOKS

For questions or comments about this book, please write to:

info@braughlerbooks.com

Braughler™
Books
braughlerbooks.com

Dedication

This book is dedicated to the Phillips Empire.
Rev. Benjamin Phillips Jr., Dr. Sharon Marie Phillips,
Isaiah Nathaniel Phillips, Michael Christian Phillips,
and everyone who has come before us, and who will
follow in our footsteps after us. This is just another
step in the foundation of our family legacy.

Contents

Preface

I must begin my book with a brief dedication to all who have helped me in this process because this truly was a team effort. This book would not be possible first and foremost without my Lord and Savior. It is because He has blessed me with this creative intuition and the experiences and obstacles put in my path that have allowed me to become the guided young man I am today. He has also blessed me with more worthwhile friends and family than I could ever need in a lifetime. Thank you to my mother, Dr. Sharon Phillips and father, Benjamin Phillips Jr. who have given me everything I have needed and asked for. When I was hungry, you provided a feast for days, when I was thirsty, you dug wells for water, and when I was lost, you mapped the entire world out to me. To my two younger brothers, Isaiah and Michael, I hope that we grow old together and stay as connected as we are now regardless of where we are in the world, and I can't wait until all our extended families meet and the Phillips Empire grows exponentially. To my brother Drew O'Donnell, I hope that God continues to bless you, even if you do not see his actions, and know that you are always an honorary Phillips, something that will never be taken lightly. Lastly, to my high school English teacher, Mrs. Kelly Dziech, thank you for tapping into my potential at such a young age and thrusting me into the fires of greatness and success. Without you, I would never have found the passion, courage, and dedication to delve into reading and writing at such a profound level as I do now.

The reasoning for this book is very simple. There are many self-help books, millionaire success secrets, and even collegiate assistance novels, but I am looking to capture all three entities in one book. A book that can be a guide to navigating the transition between high school and college, how to bring out the passion and success inside of you, and ultimately, how to be the most effective and successful person that you can be. This work is for anyone but is more actively geared to high school and collegiate students, as well as young adults in general. When people think of Millennials or teenagers everywhere, they think of rebellious, self-absorbed, obnoxious kids who are attached to their electronic devices at the hip. What if we could change that narrative and become young entrepreneurs, investors, creatives, and the next wave of generational leaders? Because essentially, we are the next population wave to dominate the workforce and lead our respective nations around the world in all aspects and industries.

I also wrote this book as a physical form of self-reflection, meditation, and self-guidance as I move forward into the impactful young adult years of my life. This reflection has allowed me to holistically analyze what has kept me on the upward and positive path since my early high school days and compile these practices into themes, steps, and characteristics that I can share with others. This is one of the keys to success that I will discuss later in the book, but I implore everyone to start writing down and documenting their experiences. Not just saving Instagram Stories or Snapchat Memories, but physically writing down what you are feeling, going through, or want to pursue. I want to shed light on what is personal success in this day and age, because it can get very convoluted especially with external influences. I also want to positively influence both those younger and older than me and step into the role as a leader that can lift others through my own personal examples. This book will include a lot of my own experiences that have influenced who I am as a young man and show why I had to mature really fast as a child. These events prompted me to always look at the world through different and multiple sets of lenses. You will see a lot of Lone Wolf Tips, which are my versions of success habits and advice that have allowed me to be successful.

What is a Lone Wolf you might ask?

Lone Wolf

I know that whenever I used to read books, I would never read the Preface or the pages before Chapter 1, because I wanted to get straight to the material. For those who are like me, I tip my hat to you, and don't hang your head because you got caught, just do me a solid and flip a couple pages back. If you are someone who read the Preface first and got to Chapter 1 the right way, then we are automatically friends now and we can arrange a time to come up with a secret handshake later. I am not writing this in case the book sells millions, but if I was able to turn the lightbulb in your head on or provide you with new information or habits to make you better than before you turned the pages of this cover, it was worthwhile. Now that we are all caught up, we can properly begin this chapter.

The Lone Wolf Method is an approach originally created by my father. I really took a full stance behind it and it has become a major part of my life, and I attribute the Lone Wolf philosophy as a factor in my own personal success. The basis for this ideology is to become your own best friend, to continue to work on yourself every single day, and to be content with taking the road less traveled to accomplish your goals. The reason I call it the Lone Wolf Method is because there isn't a lot of room for "extra stuff" or hundreds upon hundreds of friends involved in your time. This method negates any vulnerability to peer pressure, haters, and most external negativity that is always abundant in any part of your life.

The Lone Wolf is first and foremost a spiritual mantra to me. In the Bible, Genesis 49:27 states that *"Benjamin is a ravenous Wolf, in the morning he hunts his prey, and in the evening, he divides his plunder."* I interpret this scripture as the backbone of my habitual structure and daily lifestyle because I plan to attack everything I do in the beginning, with full force and the best of my ability, then reap the rewards of my hard work and dedication when I am thoroughly finished. The very last part of "dividing the plunder" to me means that I understand that I am not working for just myself. I am working to provide my family a better stress and debt free life and to show my brothers and those who look up to me the multiple avenues to success. You are going to hear me repeat this throughout the book, but the ugly side of life, especially in business, is that it is survival of the fittest and you have to have a dog-eat-dog mentality. That is why I adhere to the Lone Wolf Method, as a means of staying on top of my game in all aspects of my life, and to accomplish all that I can regardless of my age, race, or environment.

Jeff Bezos, the founder of Amazon, talks about a methodology that he lives by, and one that was the sole reason for him leaving a well-paying Wall Street job to become the richest man in the entire world. He describes his method as RMF, or Regret Minimization Framework. This means that when he reflects back on his life at 80 years old, he wants to have accomplished or at least taken a shot at, everything he ever wanted to do. This will minimize the amount of regrets that he will have over the course of his entire being. I apply this framework to my Lone Wolf Method every day because I hypothesize that synthesizing these two ideas will only further enhance myself as an entrepreneur and young businessman. I don't care that I am just nineteen and writing a book on generational success because it is something I wanted to do. I have a passion for providing help and guidance along the way to those who are in, or who will be in the same positions as myself.

. . . .

LONE WOLF TIP #1
Become a Lone Wolf

People criticize me all the time when I say I don't believe in peer pressure, but the truth is that I can't even comprehend the meaning of the subject. Your mind, body, and soul are owned 100% by YOU, and it baffles me to think that someone can even try and penetrate my mental fortress. I live by a personal rule. If it won't matter in five years, then I don't spend more than five minutes dwelling on anything or anyone who brings negative energy. Becoming mentally tough is the first stage to becoming a Lone Wolf. You will have those who seem to make it their sole mission in life to bring you down and you have to either block them out or cut them from your life. If you want to become successful at anything you do, you must remove all external negativity so that you can apply all of your energy internally. This step is difficult but necessary to be successful. The second step in becoming a Lone Wolf is critically analyzing your inner circles and the friends you house in your life. A very relevant saying is "You are who you keep around you." You don't HAVE to run with a group or posse to be "cool," especially if they aren't challenging you to be better then what you currently are. If that is the case, then it is time to become your own best friend for a time and work on finding those who support you in a healthy way in order for you to achieve your goals. The Lone Wolf Method will cause you to reevaluate your life, those who you keep around you, and how you are going to look at your future.

. . . .

This method works really well with introverted extroverts, like myself, who can be extremely social and have fun around people when they need to but work best alone and find peace and solace within the confines of their own mind, body, and soul.

I have been talking a lot about success, how to achieve it, and some initial fundamental foundation steps to actively take towards it. However, what is success? It looks different for every single person. The whole reason I can say that I am successful and can talk about the areas of success, is because I have achieved and excelled in areas that are the not the norm for a college freshman. I also have defined my own steps to success and am actively completing them one by one. There are no set guidelines for success, especially when you implement **LONE WOLF TIP #1** and block out all external negativity and societal pressures on what success is. Most people think success is having a six or seven figure salary and having luxury upon luxury at their disposal, while others view success as just at or below being financially stable in a house that contains a loving, close knit family. Success to someone who is at the very end of society's totem pole, a homeless man, could be finding a meal and being able to say, "I am successful for today."

I have given you a lot of generalized examples about what this method means to me and how I have constructed it, but I want to provide you some tangible results that it has given me when I decided to shift my mindset and commit to exponential growth and quotidian learning.

Brand Recognition: I have truly encompassed the Lone Wolf mindset in everything I do. From the book title, to the names of my workouts, or even when I write music, the Lone Wolf is reflected somehow. You will either recognize the Lone Wolf as Benjamin Phillips III and vice versa, or you will never hear about the true work that I do. This is because I work in the shadows and never let someone know what my next move is, which is reflected in one of my favorite Sun Tzu quotes. *"Let your plans be as impenetrable as night, and when you move, fall like a thunderbolt."*

Maturity: From my physical appearance, nobody would guess that I am nineteen, standing at 6'4", having a full beard, and when you hear me speak or act then you would truly not think of me as anything less than a thirty-year-old man. Implementing these steps and tips have allowed me to mature in areas of my life and business much quicker than others because of my focused approach to things and a keen sense of purpose.

Clear Mind: I have opened a lot of doors and layers in my mind to where I can have extensive communication with myself and further my deep and critical thinking skills. I have been very selective of what I choose to put in my mind, because just as I view the body as a machine for the food fuel you put inside, I view the mind as a temple as a sacred place where important things lie.

Personal Collegiate Success: I have been blessed with numerous opportunities because I worked hard and early in college to where I received my first prominent internship within three months of starting college right out of high school, and the rest built upon that. Executive positions in student organizations, highly coveted student jobs, recognition amongst the various Deans and other important professors are all a few examples of what I mean by my reality of personal collegiate success.

Purpose: A true sense of my purpose unlocked through having a clearer mind. I want to be able to be a bastion of hope and financial stability for my family, as well as be a guiding light to those around me on how to thrive in college and within the slippery slopes of life itself.

True Friends: Being a Lone Wolf allows you to have a keen sense of purpose and see other people's true intentions and their alignment of your own goals. I became very selective of using the word "friend," because I used to have a lot of "friends," now I have a lot of associates and only a few close friends that push me forward in every aspect of my life. These are the people that I can fully trust and rely on.

Those are just a few tangible things that I hope you can take away from the Lone Wolf Method in this introductory chapter. Once you understand that changing yourself for the better at any stage starts with a shift in your mindset, then you can apply action to it. These tangible items have allowed me to understand some of the early concepts of business. Being a consultant for a global firm, as well as an intern for one of the Big Four accounting firms, I have been able to learn essential business concepts and how the Lone Wolf Method can apply in Corporate America.

The first thing about business is that nobody is ever going to just give you something. Unless you are a charity, or in extreme dire situational need, business is a two-way street. I call this LEVERAGE. Don't ever go looking for handouts or what people can do for you, instead carve your own seat at the table and make people respect you and do business with you because of your actions and reputation. Leverage is the ability to supply something that someone needs in order to get what you want. For example, the head of my consulting firm, J.C. Baker, doesn't keep me on as a Junior Consultant because he only likes me or sees my potential, it is because I provide a generational bridge to our clients, as well as assist in communications and generating new leads in client acquisition for the company. I am not paid a salary or hourly wage, but I am provided the chance to have my own clients, learn from someone who has their Doctorate in business at a faster and more in-depth rate than the classroom, and network with a lot of CEO's and other C-Suite executives at major companies because of the prestige of the company, J.C. Baker & Associates.

As I said earlier, business is dog-eat-dog, so you must always stay on your toes and watch your back as a Lone Wolf. Keep your inner circle tight and always know more than your competitors know themselves. My second favorite Sun Tzu quote is *"If you know the enemy and know yourself, you need not fear the result of a hundred battles. If you know yourself but not the enemy, for every victory gained you will also suffer a defeat. If you know neither the enemy nor yourself, you will succumb in every battle."* I translate a lot of Sun Tzu, who is the author of *The Art of War* because in some instances business can be as cutthroat as war. When there are million-dollar deals on the land, consumer market share to conquest, and a global world as the battleground, business can supersede that of ordinary retail transactions in an instant.

This idea of knowing your enemy is also essential in business because you must understand that everyone is trying to figure out their own leverage they can provide, as well as what they can gain from it. This means that people will have ulterior motives and hidden agendas that you cannot be ignorant to. Donald Faison, who plays Dr. Chris Turk on the sitcom Scrubs mentions this very thing. *"If you can figure out what their motivation is, then you're ahead of the game. I think that's why a lot of people who are in this industry don't have a lot of friends - but have a lot of acquaintances - because you never know what everyone's ulterior motives are."*

This book is unique because it will cover my own personal experiences, especially in later chapters, provide Lone Wolf Tips throughout the entire novel, and also shed some insight into basic business and financial practices to provide a holistic overview on how you can really start upgrading yourself with every chapter.

Chapter Recap

KEY IDEAS

1. The Lone Wolf Methodology is a transformative process that allows the user to expand their mind, shift their focus, and help define their sense of purpose.

2. You have to dispel all external negative energy to redirect your efforts in bettering yourself internally and becoming your own best friend.

3. Business is Dog-Eat-Dog, so be a Lone Wolf and watch your own back while staying ahead of your enemies and on top of your game.

REFLECTION QUESTIONS

1. What are some things or some people that you think consist of negative energy, and how can you plan to remove them from your life?

2. What is your purpose? What are you striving hard for in life?

3. What is your own measure of success and what are some action steps that you can take to achieve it?

4. What types of leverage do you provide? How can you use your own sets of skills, connections, and experiences to achieve what you desire?

LONE WOLF TIP #1: **Become a Lone Wolf**

CHAPTER 2

Metamorphosis

For those of you who are in high school either just beginning your senior year, or counting down the days until graduation… stop. I was one of the students who couldn't wait to graduate and be off on my own in college, until I realized that in college, I had gas and insurance bills to pay, rent was due, and collegiate calculus sucked the life out of me. Don't wish away your last moments in high school, despite what everyone says, it will be the last time you interact with some of your classmates, teachers, and other faculty who you may have grown to love and appreciate over your formative years.

Some of my peers were so caught up in graduating high school that all they received was a diploma, and an empty graduation party, or an unsigned yearbook, or not even a single picture taken, or memory captured. "But Benjamin, I thought we were supposed to be Lone Wolves and thrive off being alone?" Yes, I implore you to follow the Lone Wolf Method, but don't take it to the extreme where you are a shell of your social life, you don't get involved, and you don't live for every single day. If nothing else, at least build bridges with those sitting in the desks around you, or converse with those in the cafeteria who are eating the seemingly day-old lunches with you at your table. The connections I made in high school are very dear to me, especially the teachers, because I was able to learn from their subject and personal life, and now I can talk with them on an adult level.

I was one of the students that mirrored the main character in a "High School Musical" type movie, or the principal archetype for the "all-around" teenager in high school. I was captain of the varsity Men's Basketball Team, captain of the Men's Volleyball Team, an avid lead jazz saxophonist, prominent member of the National Honors Society, and a standout 4.0 G.P.A. academic student in the Honors classes. I detail these positions not to brag or down anyone else's achievements in high school, but I say these things to show that I was intensely and innately focused even at the high school level. I was implementing aspects of the Lone Wolf Method before I had even named it and was thoroughly conscious of what I was doing.

The most applicable classes I still think about to this day, besides my English class with Kelly Dziech, were my Cooking & Baking class with Casey Haubner, where I learned how to make the best cupcakes known to man, and my Current Events class with Benjamin Zoeller, which really sparked my interest and raised my awareness on what was going on in the world around me. I say this because I understand the construct of the "High School Game" and that is why I excelled as a person and a student. In high school, you take the bus or drive to school on time, pay attention long enough to retain the right answers about the material, replicate them through homework and projects, regurgitate them through standardized tests and quizzes, and stay out of trouble while applying yourself when need be. If you follow this basic plan, then the teachers will pass you and help you thrive in other areas of your life. For example, I was showing my drive in my Current Events class enough to where Benjamin Zoeller, my teacher, had life talks with me every morning and at the end of every school day before I had basketball practice.

However, high school teaches you the basic building blocks of discipline, character, and respect, and it is fundamental that you strive to excel in every position you are placed in.

I always realized that the teachers were craving to impart knowledge beyond their assigned subject matter to students. I wish I would have connected with all my teachers in a personal manner, because building long-lasting relationships with your instructors is a complete form of success. It has been years since my freshman year of high school, but my English teacher is helping me write the book you are reading now. Here are some of the influential teachers in my high school tenure that have impacted me, and maybe you can see some similarities between them and your own teachers in their respective positions. If none of these teachers are similar to those you interact with, then go seek people like this out! They are instrumental to your success as a young adult.

Jeff Sims (Basketball Coach): I had three different varsity basketball coaches during my time at Fairfield High School, but Coach Sims was my only staple of consistency within the program throughout all three of those years. He provided me opportunities to lead, societal places to make an impact on the community, and helped me realize the world outside of basketball when I was hell-bent on becoming the next NBA or Division I star.

Jay Bauer (Volleyball Coach): I had never even thought of Men's Volleyball as a sport, much less something that I myself would participate in, however Coach Bauer pushed me beyond the edge of my own personal capacity and helped me fall in love with something I was completely ignorant about. I became a four-year varsity starter for our volleyball team and ended up winning the first school conference championship in history with him and Coach Mike Berkemeier training me.

Kelly Dziech (English Teacher): Mrs. Dziech was one of the first teachers who I felt genuinely cared about me and brought out my true potential as a creative writer and avid reader. She wasn't scared to push me well past my intellectual limits and ended up being a secondary mother figure in my life as someone I could confide in and trust.

Benjamin Zoeller (Current Events Teacher): Mr. Zoeller was the first male teacher that I could open up to and talk about sports, politics, and other young adult stuff because he could relate to me and my level. He really helped develop my budding question-first mentality to everything that was happening in the world and helped me a lot in the transition between high school and college.

Elizabeth Gladish (Spanish Teacher): Senora Gladish was my one and only Spanish teacher who I became close with after really taking a liking to Spanish culture and the language after the first class level. She was a no-nonsense, straight-forward teacher who pushed me to participate in the school's annual fishing trip for students with disabilities. This was a life changing event because it broadened my horizons on different types of children and what they go through, and to be appreciative of life in so many different aspects.

Casey Haubner (Cooking Teacher): Casey Haubner was always there to have some leftovers from her cooking class when I needed a quick bite to eat before practice and was someone I could be my authentic self with. I would always be the clown in her class, within reason, and she would allow me to have fun and experiment with the recipes.

My reason for detailing all of these wonderful people is not so you transfer to my high school in Fairfield, Ohio and take their courses, it is to demonstrate that educational relationships can expand beyond the classroom if you have the initiative and presence to do so. Teachers are there to educate not only their subject material but provide guidance in maneuvering the slippery slopes of life in general. Never take a class or teacher for just the surface level expectations, because you never know what may come out of that relationship if you provide your authenticity, your purpose, and your leverage to that relationship. I have been able to receive many letters of recommendation, scholarship opportunities, and life advice from my teachers by cultivating these relationships in a genuine way.

It is easy to succumb to not caring or trying your hardest in high school when you realize the true realistic nature of the public education system. However, without realizing it, this is one of your first major obstacles in life. How to apply yourself to the best of your ability, exceed among the rest of the entire school, and how to get involved and build your LEVERAGE, all while within the confines of a subsequent, lazy atmosphere or environment. I am not trying to criticize all high schools in the nation, but what I am saying is, I don't believe most high schools prepare you to perform and excel at the collegiate level and fail to teach you to critically think and develop high emotional quotient capability.

Despite this, I don't want you to get a pessimistic outlook on life when you're in high school because the experiences and extracurriculars I participated in were stepping stones to who I have become. Let's deeply look at the tail-end of my high school career and analyze the positives.

National Honor Society: I participated in a host of community service events such as funding to send an international student to school, packing supplies for the homeless, and assisting in nursing homes with their elderly patients. This taught me how to work within a system and how to coexist with people who have different work habits or learning structures than me.

Captain of Varsity Basketball and Volleyball Team: This was where the bulk of my management and persevering skill sets originally came from. I learned how to be a leader, what my leadership style is, how to be the liaison between players and coaches, and how to humbly be the face of the team. This set up the earliest individual systems and processes for my business skills such as: Project Management, Efficiency, Relationship Building, and understanding the Levels of Communication.

Jazz Saxophonist & Piano Player: This was my creative outlet as an appreciative fan of the contemporary arts. I have always loved Miles Davis and Gregory Porter, as well as other jazz musicians, and old school R&B artists such as Luther Vandross and Stevie Wonder. My musical taste has a direct influence on my personal style and genre of who I am as a young black man. I would always love to sing in the shower, and secretly wished that I would've explored choir in high school because I have a real passion for music. One day when I was around 13 or 14, I decided to sing for my family and friends at a holiday gathering on the piano, and I remember my father telling me that I was not good and to stop trying to sing. I ran downstairs and cried myself to sleep because I didn't think I was good enough. Through getting older I realized that it wasn't about what anyone else thought, it was about me being free and doing something I loved.

People could never figure me out in high school, students and faculty both. I was a basketball playing, music loving, anime geekin, computer nerdin' boy who never really seemed to fully assimilate into one clique. I also had to deal with the whole biracial paradox of being "too white" for the black kids, and being "too black" for the white kids, all while not even having a chance to represent the Filipino blood that also is a part of who

I am. This was a personal struggle for me early on, but I realized that it was to my advantage. Much like having a diversified stock portfolio, which we will cover later, I had a diversified portfolio of friend groups that I could engage with in a genuine way, without consequence of personal image or reputation. I would rave about the Pokemon I had just captured in my video game to my nerd friends, write music and record covers with my musical friends, and then be blessed to play for the entire school on Friday nights and slam-dunk a basketball while the crowd went crazy. I also didn't believe in the whole "cool kids" persona of high schoolers, because most of the time they ended up working for the nerds and the geeks they bullied in high school. Dispel all myths you have surrounding the world "cool" and instead replace it with the word "successful," because this is what truly matters after high school.

It is extremely important to know who has your back when things get rough or when you need a helping hand in life. Things in high school pop up for the first time that you aren't prepared for because you are just starting out in this journey, but try to find those key figures in your life who are there for you. Whether you are struggling in a class, not having enough money to eat lunch, made a mistake and got in trouble at school, or you became an early parent or find yourself metaphorically drowning in life, you need to understand that you are not in it alone.

LONE WOLF TIP #2:
Finding Your Support System

Going through anything alone is a daunting task but is sometimes not the best course of action. It is impossible for you to know every outcome of every action you do or partake in, and it is seemingly impossible to know exactly how you are going to progress through the future. However, if you have a support system around you to help pick you up when you fall, guide you when you are lost, and also be a shoulder to cry on from time to time, then you are in good company. "It takes a village to raise a child" is a popular quote that seamlessly intertwines itself with this **LONE WOLF TIP** because when you align yourself with God, family, close friends, and mentors, you will find the journey of life to be much more meaningful and a tad bit easier. During high school, my family and girlfriend at the time, Autumn Murphy, as well as my teammates and teachers comprised the basis of my support system.

For those of you currently in high school, pay attention to what I am about to say. I am going to give you the three tips on how to be successful in the current environment you are in right now.

1. **Learn Time-Management:** Learning how to balance extracurriculars with your regular school schedule leads to beneficial time-management skills. Prioritization is key in any facet of life that you go through.

2. **Develop a Competitive Edge:** Finding what you are good at or passionate about is fantastic, but finding someone who has similar interests early allows you to strengthen your game. I live by a saying that says "iron sharpens iron," which means that if you keep good company around you who are pushing you, you will upgrade yourself unconsciously.

3. **Apply Yourself:** You are in high school, not retiring from your career yet. You are literally in the beginning stages of your young adult life, because everything you do in high school will either have a positive or negative impact on the rest of your high school experience, your collegiate experience, and be the building blocks into adulthood. Make sure to apply to

every scholarship you can find, if college is where you want to go post-high school, because these are instrumental in alleviating financial stress in college.

Once you understand these basic concepts, you will be able to understand how I took my high school experience a step further. High school is where I saw the seeds of my entrepreneurial passion sown. During basketball season, we held a fundraiser every year for the varsity team selling our themed shirts so we could raise money for our travel suits. My first year on varsity during my sophomore year, I outsold everyone on the entire team, in the history of the program, and nobody has beaten my record ever since. All of my teammates were so mad when they would talk to students and potential customers because they would say, "I already sold it to the tall, cute light-skin boy" or "I already bought five for my entire family because of Ben."

While the people on my team were selling individually to every single person, I was selling bundles. Family bundles, the entire girls soccer team from the 7th grade all the way to the 12th grade, substitute teachers, the surrounding elementary schools, I was selling to everyone. I even went so far as to implement the early stages of social media marketing by posting them on my Instagram and Snapchat, tagging and highlighting those who had bought from me already, making them post it on their pages, and then have people who followed them contact me about buying shirts. I am pretty sure I even sold one or two shirts to neighboring high schools, just because of my friends and contacts over there.

This business skill of dominating sales practices was something I learned early on, especially the rule of "people do business with who they know and like." When the basketball team would get their boxes of shirts to pass out to their customers, some people would get one or two boxes, but there had to be an entire car full of boxes for my account. This plan backfired on me because then I had to personally hand out every single shirt that I had sold, but I won a gym bag with my name and number embroidered on it, so I was extremely proud of myself.

No matter how hard you work and strive for success, there will always be things out of your control. During the summer of my junior year in high school, my father got into a near fatal motorcycle accident. He was driving 70 mph and got hit by a car that didn't see him in the turning lane and flew out of his bike high in the air and hit the ground and rolled a good 12 feet away. Now, my father is around 6'7 and 300lbs, so he is a big man, but he also has had numerous back surgeries in his life, along with decades of strain from playing professional basketball overseas. This sent a shocking chill down my spine that left me in temporary paralysis when my Mom called me and told me the news as she was speeding to the hospital. It was at this moment where I had my first realization that life can be snuffed out in an instant. Fifty years of experiences, love, and passion could all be eradicated within moments.

He survived the accident but had to be placed in a rehabilitation center for around 2 months while his body healed, and I became the de facto head of the Phillips house. With my mother, two younger brothers, and two grandparents all living in one house without our leader, I had to grow up very quickly at 17 years old. My mom, Dr. Sharon Phillips, is a child psychologist and has her own practice which meant that she worked long hours. I had to take care of my brothers and grandparents while also studying for the upcoming ACT and participating in summer basketball camps and practices every day. I had to be trained in home Peritoneal Dialysis for my Nana because she had recently been put on dialysis treatment, and I had to go through an extensive training that my father was going to go through before his accident. I will never forget that time because it showed me that at the end of the day, family and faith are the two things I can always lean on no matter what. You do whatever you need to for family, no excuses, no selfishness, and you do it because it is your duty and your job.

Being entrusted daily with the actual physical health of another person as a teenager is one of the things that accelerated my maturity level early because these are real life scenarios which nobody really can prepare for. In business it is the same way, you must be prepared for the unexpected in any situation. Whether a stock falls drastically, international trade talks are volatile, or a personal situation affects your work life, these are all things that we have to be ready to accommodate at any time, and critically think on how to work around them.

Another devastating blow happened the summer before I entered college. It was the passing of my grandfather, who is the origin of my namesake and my father before me. I have always had a strange relationship with death because it seems in my family that I am the one it first encounters. I was the one who found our first dog dead on our sidewalk when I was around 12 years old. I remember how lifeless and how cold his body was, and how I even felt myself start to shiver.

I also was the first one who found my grandfather dead in his favorite chair in my grandparents' room. I had woken up to fix them breakfast like I did every morning, and he just wouldn't respond to my call for some reason. When I went into his room his body was cold, his eyes were open but never blinking, and his body was as stiff as a board. There was no breath coming out of his body and I just kept waiting on him to tell me to fix him breakfast. After that I remember the bestial screams of my grandmother calling him to come back and answer her, as well as seeing my father trying to resuscitate him, but when the ambulance came and saw that rigor mortis had already set in, the man had confirmed it with a single glance. It was the first time I had seen my father shed a tear. My mother was very helpful in guiding us through this transition because that is what she wrote her dissertation on: Bereavement in African American Families and Communities. These experiences heightened my maturity level and allowed me to look at the world and life in a more appreciative way.

This was where I understood the meaning of true friendship, and where Drew O'Donnell became an honorary member of the Phillips Empire, bestowed by me as the next head in the Phillips lineage. Drew attended the funeral and sat with my brothers and I and helped carry the casket from the funeral building to the vehicle. This is where I realized that this was someone who was more than an ordinary friend and knew that we would be there for each other no matter what, and that the looming presence of going away for college would only strengthen our bond.

The college search is one that every parent either dreads or loves, because of the traveling, the emotions, and the tightening of their financial belts. My very first choice was the Massachusetts Institute of Technology (MIT) and my original plan involved me going to play basketball there and study politics and law. I remember being flown out to campus for a basketball camp and how I dunked in the very first drill and made the structure of the entire basket shake. The coaches automatically were impressed and wanted me to come there, but it just wasn't in my favor financially and academically. This was one of my first major personal losses and rejections, and I felt like I wouldn't go anywhere if I couldn't get into MIT. But using my support system from my family (**LONE WOLF TIP #2**) I was able to bounce back with reignited vigor. My second choice was Georgetown University in D.C., and they flew me and my father out and we toured the campus. This was actually my dream school since I was a child. I wanted to study law at Georgetown and then become President. (It was that simple in my head.) I got accepted to the school but again, couldn't afford it financially and my dreams came crashing down again. I had been accepted to the Miami University Farmer School of Business already but scoffed at the idea of going to school thirty minutes away from home to Oxford, Ohio. Quick shout out to the Fairfield City School District, the men of Alpha Phi Alpha Fraternity Incorporated, and the men of Kappa Alpha Psi Fraternity Incorporated for providing me scholarships to further my education at a higher level. It turned out to be the best decision I have ever made. It is because of Michelle Thomas, the Director for Diversity & Inclusion at FSB, that I enrolled at the university and felt extremely comfortable. She became another mother figure to me while on campus, and I often call her Mama Thomas. Little did I know that this decision would open doors I didn't even know existed, and where the journey of my life would fully start to take off.

Chapter Recap

KEY IDEAS

1. Capitalize on every opportunity in high school, and if you feel like there is none around you, go and make one happen. Examples could be: Student clubs, sports teams, community service, employment.

2. Build strong rapport with your teachers and stay in touch over the years because you never know who people know. Also, the more bridges you build, the easier it is to get places.

3. Your support system is very foundational to your success and your growth as a human being in every field.

REFLECTION QUESTIONS

1. Who are some teachers that you really like? Find out where they went to college, their hidden talents, get to know them genuinely and personally.

2. What is a time during high school where you felt you were backed up against the wall, and how did you overcome it?

3. What colleges are you applying to and dream of getting accepted into?

4. Who are the people who make up your support system and why?

LONE WOLF TIP #2: **Finding Your Support System**

CHAPTER 3

Tabula Rasa

All my life I have been on the quest for knowledge and have had a hunger for gained intellect. At first, that revolved completely around books and the fantastic worlds and messages inside them. I loved the grandeur experience it gave me to turn every page in a novel I was completely engrossed in. I read everything from fiction books to autobiographies, and really craved the physical experience of holding hardcovers and paperbacks between my hands. I thought that I knew everything there was in the world and was at the age in my life where I thought I was "grown" because I was going off to college. I was no different than every other kid arriving to campus for the first time and being hit with culture shock.

You may be wondering why I named this title "Tabula Rasa," or even wondering what it means, and even I didn't know until I researched it and starting writing about it. Tabula Rasa is essentially the philosophical concept of a blank slate, where we are all born without true content in our heads, and that it only comes from perception and experience. John Locke, a staple of the Enlightenment era, wrote *"That it is the freedom of individuals to author their own soul."* I applied this idea to my entrance into the realm of higher education at Miami University, not because I was an infant with no mental capacity, but because I knew little else about the world besides the four walls of my home, and the four walls of my high school.

I was somewhat sheltered as a kid because I had strong, loving, and (sometimes) overprotective parents. However, I did come out of high school in the top tenth percentile of my class of around 800, didn't have any kids or anything criminal on my record, and was accepted to a top tier business school with a plethora of scholarships. At least this is the argument that my parents gave when I asked why I wasn't allowed to "hang out" much in high school, which was a positive thing for me, and I will forever thank them for raising me well.

When I first opened the door to my dorm, everything changed. For the first time in my life I was away from home in a setting like this, had a place to call my own, was mostly independent financially, and had to associate with a whole new world of people. When I say a whole new world, I literally meant that there were students in my building from India, Peru, Japan, and China that spoke different languages, and all had unique backgrounds, but we were all united by a common understanding that we were students at the same university together at the same time. I met different students from inner cities, rural areas, and a myriad of socioeconomic backgrounds. Some students were the children of the CEO's of major banks and companies, and some literally came from the "ghettos" across the nation. This situation opened my eyes and expanded my horizons on learning and culture. The opportunity to live in different environments, join different collegiate clubs and organizations, and explore different relationships at different levels than my high school years, are all things that were new and exciting to me. That is why I begin with Tabula Rasa. There was an empty blank slate for me as I entered college and here is where the real change of my mindset started to transpire, and with it, the birth of the Lone Wolf.

I had met my roommate, Jalen Warren, through a mutual friend of ours, and he connected us through Facebook. We seemed to hit off pretty well on a surface level. We were both young black men: He wanted to be a doctor and I wanted to be a businessman, and we also both played basketball and were team captains at our respective schools. He was from Cleveland, so I didn't actually meet him until we both got into the dorm. It was just one of those moments when you sensed something special was in the air. I had a best friend, ultimate rival, and someone who genuinely wanted me to excel in life academically and financially.

To all of the students who will be entering college soon, or even if you are in college, or you are transferring, a big portion of your time in your initial years will be shared with your roommate. Whether you get along with them or not is irrelevant, but because you share a living space together, you will have to learn to be an adult and compromise. From my experience, it is a lot better to get along with your roommate, and even better for them to become your best friend, but don't be scared if that is not your case because it isn't the end of the world.

Just because you have been living your life a certain way doesn't mean you have to change who you are in your dorm to appease someone else, but you have to take a personal inward reflection about your habits because college dorms are small. So, if you are a messy and unorganized person, try to pair up with a messy roommate, or if you are an OCD clean freak like myself, try to pair up with someone who is like that.

If I could point to a single thing that made me successful my first year in college as a freshman, it would be the fact that I was literally the best dressed man on campus. Again, I am not saying this in terms of braggadocio, but I made it part of my competitive edge to look the best that I could be in every business environment. Every single time I would walk into my business school for a meeting or class, I would throw one of my suits on. At first people would turn their heads and wonder if I was a professor or grad student because of the way I carried myself.

At the beginning of freshman year when classes started, I was late to one of my very first classes. The professor just so happened to be running a tad bit late as well, but the majority of the students were there in a big classroom. I walked in with my suit on and my bag around my shoulder and headed towards the front, because that is where I like to sit anyways, and that is where the only available seat was. As soon as I walked in, the chatter quieted down, and people started taking out their laptops and uncapping their pens eagerly looking towards me. I thought it was because I was the only black male in the class, and that I was the test subject in a case study or something, but someone said, "Good Morning Professor," and I introduced myself as Benjamin Phillips III…Freshman Finance Student. Everyone started laughing and then the professor came in a few moments after and quieted everyone down to begin the lesson.

Towards the middle and tail-end of the semester I was still wearing my suits, and people started talking how they usually do when they do not understand something. "Who does this freshman think he is?," "Who is he trying to impress?," and "We get it you are a business student, chill out and stop being self-absorbed." Little did they realize that I was already blocking out external negativity, and that I wasn't wearing my suits to impress anyone, besides the cute upperclassman girls sometimes, but I was wearing my suits because it was my form of armor. Just as I wore the full armor of God every day derived from Ephesians 6:11, putting my suit on changed my mindset and the perception of myself. I started seeing myself as a successful businessman, I paid more attention in class, and I carried myself with confidence and swagger that all complimented my Lone Wolf agenda.

Another main reason I wore my suits was because they were the last gift my father gave me before I left for college. I remember him saying that every man needs to own a suit, and you need to understand that you are a man with or without it on, but great suits compliment great men. "You always have to stay fresh in case GQ comes knocking on your door" as he said with one of his famous smirks. Most of the time when I go out in public, even if it is to the mall or store, I just throw my suit on because it is the international symbol for business. Business can be global, national, or even local, and that is why I choose to look my best whenever I can because you never know when opportunity will strike. In the famous words of Will Smith "If you stay ready, you ain't gotta get ready."

This method is how I landed my highly coveted student job with the Farmer School of Business Dean's Suite. The Farmer School of Business at Miami University is an institution that shines above the rest. From the very first semester I had to undergo the "Business Core" which consisted of foundational business practices, professional writing, creativity and entrepreneurship, and basic coding. This was the first time I was academically challenged, and is a testament to FSB, on what they expect from even their freshman students. The expectations were already high, so I knew I had to work extremely hard and separate myself as the Lone Wolf from the rest of the pack.

I had never explored the top floor of my business school and I just decided to venture up there, with my black suit on and a red tie, and explore. I ended up walking into the Dean's office and I remember saying "Hi, I am a freshman and I have never been up here, so I wanted to see who you guys are." I was taken on a mini-tour around the Dean's Suite and met all of the powerful people who run the business school because of my curiosity.

The engrained image of the well-dressed freshman who had the effrontery to waltz in the Dean's Suite remained in their head when they were recruiting for their highly selective student assistant position. I became the student liaison between the business school and the copious amount of Fortune 500 companies and high-profile individuals who visited, which increased my global network exponentially. The dress code for the job was business casual, which happens to not be in my vocabulary, but I always wore my suit and tie. When international visitors or professors would come, I would be looking my best because I was one of the first faces they saw as they walked into the office, and I was complimented regularly on my appearance, which increased my standing with those in the Dean's Suite. The initial curiosity excursion also landed me a role at the end of the year when I was featured in a new FSB media production, where they highlighted one standout senior and one standout freshman to follow around campus with a camera crew and shoot a professional video about their time so far at Miami. The title of the video was "Farmer School: Beyond Ready," and when that finished video went public on YouTube, my stock in the business school started to rise. This really cemented my progress and was the icing on the cake for a successful freshman year. This led to most of all the professors and top faculty to know my name and who I was, which proved to be very beneficial in terms of vertical networking.

I knew that Miami was the right choice for me because within three months of enrollment, I was able to land a major internship with one of the Big Four accounting firms in the nation. This was because within the very first few weeks on the semester starting, I joined Michelle Thomas's student org and got involved right away. The name of the organization was called the Multicultural Business Association (MBA), I eventually became the Treasurer of it my freshman year, and the group's main goal was focused on professional development for its members. I attended resume and networking workshops, how to work on my elevator pitch, and how to revamp my LinkedIn professionally. I especially learned how important it was to network HORIZONTALLY, and not just VERTICALLY. What I mean by that is, you need to network extensively with your peers and those around you on the same playing field as you because these are the people who will comprise the next generation of leaders when you rise. Yes, it is important to establish connections with recruiters and C-Suite individuals, but keep in mind that the next CEO, founder, president, or doctor could be next to you in Accounting or Biology class. All of this understanding made me a holistically, polished student, and even though I didn't have the experience of other jobs, internships, or club involvement, job recruiters were able to see the potential in me when I went to our school's Career Fair, which we will talk more about in the next chapter.

You may be thinking "Man did this guy even have any type of fun in college?" And the answer is that I would need to write another book on my full adventures in college with Jalen and my other college friends, but that material would never get published. Don't get me wrong I had an abundance of fun and parties at the bars, houses, and signature events, but I knew that I was at college for a purpose and I stayed true to my spiritual mantra of Genesis 49:27.

. . . .

LONE WOLF TIP #3
Think Years Ahead

One of the sayings I hate is "Just Live In the Moment." I don't hate this saying because I am a pessimist who doesn't enjoy the day. I do truly take time to fully enjoy every minute and hour that

I am given every day. I really just hate when people say this and use it as an excuse to completely derail their life plans, use it as a free pass to make stupid mistakes, and expect this notion of YOLO (You Only Live Once) to serve as the exemplified life they should live in college. How about instead of all of that, you become the ARCHITECT of your own life, by LIVING in the PRESENT, but also PLANNING for the FUTURE. I always relate life to a chess and not a checkers game, because this is a long-term deal where you have to think of your life 4-5 moves ahead, or else life itself will decide those moves for you. Whether that is financially, physically, or emotionally, I would rather choose to maintain the control over my life that is in my hands, and not blame others or a younger version of myself for not taking life seriously until I needed to.

. . . .

Planning ahead was very instrumental in me landing my internship because my friend who had similar interests also landed an internship with the same company his freshman year as well. His name is Kyle Broadnax, and because of him, my mentor Azieb Zeray, as well as Akosua Boadi-Agyemang, I had the tools and the knowledge to cultivate a positive relationship with the company recruiters and excel in the interviews. They helped guide me through Career Fair, which is a large event held at most universities, where hundreds of companies come and try to find the top students that fit their company and provide them internships or full-time job offers. Whether you are a business major or not, everyone in every industry needs to have a sense of professional development in order to pursue their careers and aspirations. One huge tip that I can express to college students before I cover my internship process and Career Fair in the next chapter is that you will always have a voice, even as a freshman. What freshman, and even sophomores, can do when they talk to recruiters, is recount their standout high school events, as well as any new experiences in college so far, because people love to see that you are getting involved early.

I started compiling experiences on top of experiences the rest of freshman year. Students, don't think that freshman year is the year to get acclimated to everything, be passive to opportunities, and just say that I'll apply myself when I am ready sophomore year. That is what the first month or two of college is for, and you are able to accomplish and achieve whatever you put your mind to, because college is the hot-bed of opportunity. People want you to try new things, explore new places, and join new clubs you never thought you would ever join. Stepping out of your comfort zone is one of the biggest strategies to success in college, because you don't know what you don't know, and the worst thing that can happen is that you tried something new but just didn't like it.

I was able to take an all-expenses-paid trip to Washington D.C. with the Government Relations Network at Miami, led by Randi Thomas, where I got to network with politicians, tour famous museums, and even sit in Rep. John Lewis's office. I was invited to the Miami Business Advisory Council luncheon, where I got to meet and network with some extremely successful and powerful people who all share the title of Miami alumni. During Black History Month in February, I was invited to the local church to speak about whatever I wanted, and this was my first entrance into formal public speaking. I spoke about Tulsa, Oklahoma and the power of Black Wall Street, as well as money management and financial literacy. These few stand-out experiences my freshman year were what led me to develop as a person because I was all over the place, and I said yes to everything. Little did I know that I was actively promoting my personal brand with everything I did.

. . . .

LONE WOLF TIP #4
Don't Build A Brand

You are probably looking at that tip and are just now scratching your head wondering what I even meant by that. It is an interesting juxtaposition but is something that I realized even when I was playing basketball in high school. This **LONE WOLF TIP** is something I live by because it coexists cohesively with my leadership style. Don't focus on trying to actively build a brand, and instead let the brand build itself. What's understood doesn't need to be explained. I didn't need to go around telling people I was the varsity basketball captain, people already knew because of what my teammates said, how I carried myself, and how the coaches spoke highly of me. Do HIGH QUALITY work and let your brand organically foster and speak for itself. For example, I went and created my own business cards and had them printed and sent to my dorm, which I carried around in my wallet and business card case. So now instead of my perception being a freshman who is a Finance student, it went from here is a young businessman who wears a suit every day and has his own business cards. Other students thought I was crazy and being "extra" when I showed them to people. The CEO's of companies and the job recruiters didn't think I was being "extra" when they handed me their business cards and I handed mine right back. This relayed the message that I was someone who knew how to maneuver in this industry and legitimize my brand. There is a reason you see commercials for all sorts of cars in every make and model, but you never see a commercial on TV trying to sell you a Lamborghini or Ferrari, because they know their brand is built on such a high pedestal, that it speaks for itself. There is no point in advertising and marketing their cars when it is understood that they are luxury vehicles. Let's start making luxury brands and not focus so much on promotion in this context, but doing high quality work, always staying ready, (like Will Smith) and leading by example.

. . . .

A lot of my peers and colleagues were very excited when I told them about this book and were helpful in providing a holistic set of general college tips that I thought I should share with you in the conclusion of this chapter.

- **Don't get caught up in the hype:** There are always going to be parties, events, and functions that I implore you to go and enjoy this part of your youth to the fullest but remember your purpose for being at college. It isn't to drink the night away, be caught up in social clubs or Greek Life, or even take your independence to unfathomable levels by staying up all night every night playing video games. You are there for a reason.

- **Establish a personal balance of work, school, and social time:** College is different than high school, you won't be able to play the "High School Game" with these college professors. Classes are mainly papers, projects, a few quizzes, two exams, and one final. There are not a lot of buffer points like high school. For every credit hour you have in a collegiate course, you want to study 2-3 hours outside of class for it. Make sure that you allot time to your studies, your social life, and if you are employed when you are in school. This is where your time-management skills come into play!

- **Utilize Office Hours:** These are select times that professors have their doors open for any questions or extra help outside of the allotted class period. Even if you don't have a question, go to these office hours and try to befriend and get to know your professor, they are human beings too! It could be the difference between a B- and an A, or they could be the bridge to your next internship or job offer.

- **Find your study method:** I work best when I study alone once I understand the material, but before that I work best with groups because someone either knows the answer or can explain it in terms I understand. Don't be ashamed to get a personal tutor. Most universities have tutoring services that are either faculty or other students who extensively know the material and are there for a reason. During class sit in the front row and turn your phone off to fully engage. The reality is, if you miss one class, or start to zone out in your classes, you're missing valuable material that YOU ARE PAYING FOR, so you might as well educate yourself and pay attention. Even if you are struggling in the class, at least the instructor knows you are trying your best and will be more likely to help!

- **Finals Week:** Yes, Finals Week can be exactly what you thought it was, students pulling all-nighters and surviving off Red Bull and diner hamburgers. This does not have to be your reality however. Start studying a week in advance of Finals week, and schedule time to study each subject with plenty of breaks included. Find those who have an A in the class, go to office hours, and GET SOME SLEEP. I would wear my suit for every final that I had, because I found that it would place me in a more focused state, and allowed me to attack the final with a renewed sense of purpose, I dressed for what I predicted the outcome to be: successful, instead of showing up with sweats on and my espresso two minutes before the exam started.

- **Explore anything that piques your interest:** You have heard me say it throughout this entire chapter, but college is a place where resources and opportunity meet at the intersection of YOU. Join an E-Sports club because you think you may want to try gaming or go backpacking in the Bahamas with the Rec Center club because it is a cheap trip over winter break. Whatever it is, step out of your comfort zone to try new things. Sir Richard Burton says that "The gladdest moment in human life, me thinks, is a departure into unknown lands." Explore your different friend groups, try new food, and get out into the world.

- **You are not confined to your freshman major:** I can't stress this enough that I am confident your major, or a subset of what you think you want to do, will change. I thought I was going into politics and law my entire life until I got to college and decided on business. Even in business I switched from Economics coming in, to Finance, and who knows if that is what I will ultimately graduate with. Obviously stay on track with your academic advisors, counselors, and teachers to graduate on time and with the correct amount of credits but find what you are passionate in AND what can sustain you in a career, because this is YOUR life.

- **Learn about yourself:** Take the time to really find out who you are, who you want to be, and where you have come from. It's OK to not be OK sometimes, it's perfectly fine to cry, be emotional, express yourself. Make your MENTAL HEALTH a priority. You know what you are dealing with and how you are feeling, don't let anyone tell you different. I don't recommend missing multiple classes and lectures, but if you need to take a personal day to rest, relax, and reenergize yourself, then by all means go ahead. Just don't do it on a day you have an important project or test to take care of.

- **Understand that your home life may change:** It is funny that a lot of times when college students go home for the first time after being in college for a while, the original home seems a bit different. Your room may have been taken over by a sibling, it won't feel the same because you have been used to your college dorm, or some other family matters might have happened while you were gone. My father decided to move my youngest brother Michael down to Florida to focus on Division I basketball and pursue his dreams, so my parents and family were all still together, but half of the Phillips Empire was on the opposite bottom end of the country. This made for a complete familial shift when I returned home, and we had to have some holidays and family meetings through Facetime video conferencing and phone calls. However, just know that if your family bond is strong and is blessed by the Lord, it can overcome anything.

• **"College is the best years of your life" is a myth:** I say this statement is a myth because college is definitely a memorable time, and you will have friends and contacts for the rest of your life from school, but it is a short period of the course of your entire life. There won't be another time where you will be in an environment like college with people in your age range and sharing similar interests, all exploring the same life changes as you. However, I believe that college contained some very life-changing and fun years, but if these are the best years of my life then what else do I have to look forward too? I live by the philosophy that whatever present year I am in is the best year of my life, because I am never going to stop maximizing the value in myself and my experiences. Don't get caught in the college bubble and never want to leave, because there is a whole world to explore outside of university. Even though you may graduate, you never stop learning.

Chapter Recap

KEY IDEAS

1. Understand that college is a completely different beast than high school, and you have to truly apply yourself and expect to be challenged.

2. Networking HORIZONTALLY is just as important as networking VERTICALLY.

3. Plan for the FUTURE not the PRESENT, and let your brand organically foster based upon the high-quality work you do.

REFLECTION QUESTIONS

1. What are the study habits that work best for you? How can you be a better student in this area?

2. What are some ways you can improve your own personal brand? Do you make sure that everything you do is completed to the fullest extent and highest quality of work?

3. Do you have a plan written down for your future? If so, how are you going to go about accomplishing it?

4. Do you have external negativity in your life from haters? How are you expelling that negativity and focusing on yourself?

LONE WOLF TIP #3: **Think Years Ahead**

LONE WOLF TIP #4: **Don't Build A Brand**

CHAPTER 4

Sink or Swim

"What doesn't kill you makes you stronger" is a quote that I believe is extremely applicable in business. Like I have been saying this entire novel, business is dog-eat-dog, and it's best to be a Lone Wolf. This is how I felt when I went to my first Career Fair at my university. I thought it would be fun to attend, look at companies, and see how I stacked up against everyone around me, but the experience was nothing like I thought it would be. When I walked into our collegiate basketball arena, where the event was held, I felt like I was on the floor of the New York Stock Exchange. There were lines as long as amusement park rides, students running around with nervous and anxious looks on their faces, and there was a constant hum of chatter and small talk throughout the entire venue.

When I walked through the entrance of the building, I was in awe of the function, and that must have given away that I was a freshman. One of the event planners pulled me to the side to give me a layout of everything and a brief overview, and I remember asking him why so many people looked like they were going to explode or hide in a corner. He explained that most of these students are juniors and seniors and are looking for their last internship or a full-time job, it was a sink or swim environment. That took some pressure off me because I knew that my future didn't solely depend on this Career Fair my freshman year.

During Career Fair the main thing that everyone told me was that the larger companies don't even bother with freshman, and it was a waste of time to even talk to them because you won't get an internship anyway. This came from some professors and mostly other students who had been previously. Once you realize that a lot of people's external negative energy stems from their own fears and failures, you can start to disregard it and focus on your Lone Wolf mentality. Truly understanding the haters and their behavior is what allows you to take control of the situation and can empower you to reach new heights that people have never seen before. I went up to a copious amount of companies that, through conversation seemed to be very interested in me, and they didn't even know I was a freshman until they asked at the very end because they wanted to hire me on, unfortunately couldn't because they said they were looking for older candidates.

I stopped at my number one choice after I had a few conversations under my belt and approached them with confidence and a dash of humility and was expedited up the lines because of some students I knew were working the booths. I was shepherded to the main recruiter and she already knew of me. This comes back around to my earlier statement of networking horizontally because, unbeknownst to me, some of my mentors and older friends mentioned my name to the recruiters in a favorable way. So I was already expected, which made the process easier. I was granted an on-campus interview with the company and aced that one, after which I was moved along to the final interview at the actual company building.

I was so nervous because I was going to have three consecutive interviews, one with a manager, senior manager, and a partner. My father drove me to downtown Cincinnati where the office was located, and I brought my roommate, Jalen, along for moral support, highlighting and cementing the fact that he was a true friend. I knew the day was going to go well when my first interview consisted of nothing but basketball, and we hit it off perfectly to the point where he invited me to the company basketball games every week.

There is a saying that real business is done on the golf course. This means that a lot of businessman play golf and use it as a form of conversation because the games are usually invite-only. They are comfortable on the field, and they can speak in a more relaxed environment than the office. I would refute that saying by declaring that business is decided by who you are trying to do business with, and the environment that they are involved in. You never know what someone's hypothetical "golf course" is and I happened to connect with my interviewer through basketball, which led to invite-only games, and I started building rapport with those in the company as well.

The second interview had me sweating on the inside because this was a more serious interview, and I had to talk about something I had no idea about, AI & Robots. I knew that I was confident in myself to discuss anything and hold my own in a conversation, so my main strategy was to turn the questions back on him and let him explain what he knew, and I could pull more content and questions from the bulk of his talking, and this strategy worked in my favor. He proclaimed that I was the best interviewee so far that knew of this industry in depth and was able to talk to him on a professional level. I quickly shook his hand, stepped outside, and gave a thumbs up to the big man upstairs and let out a sigh of relief. My third interview was basically a recap and review of the company, and was more of just getting to know me, which was quickly proceeded by lunch paid for by the business, and then the conclusion of the day.

I met up with my father and Jalen to debrief and they were

really excited. The next day the recruiter called and told me I had the internship and she was really impressed with what the senior manager said. I graciously accepted and then called my family to have a Phillips Scream-On-The-Phone session about my success. This is what jump started the beginning of my collegiate success and proved that my Lone Wolf Method was starting to bear the fruits of my labor. My friends were proud and were happy for me as well, and my name quickly spread around the business school as another freshman who got a big-time internship offer.

During my Multicultural Business Association meeting, we did a quick recap of how everyone's Career Fairs went, starting from seniors, and then trickling down to freshman. Some seniors were still going through their full-time interview process, juniors were excited about either continuing the internships they already had or were also in the interview process, and sophomores were detailing the companies they had spoken too and wanted to follow up with next year or so. When it came to the freshman, I didn't really want to say my news, but the co-President Imani Steele, prompted me to share. I stood up and told everyone I had accepted my offer to intern with one of the Big Four accounting firms, and everyone started clapping loudly and were genuinely proud of me. When I scanned the room, there were a few that seemed like either they didn't fully understand or didn't care, and I learned a very important lesson.

You have to pay attention to those who don't clap when you succeed because people love to see you do well, but never better than themselves. Genuine people who are happy for you will show it, and the same is also for those who are not happy for you. With the excitement of the internship offer also came a lot of critics and misanthropists. People were saying the only reason that I got the internship was because I was a freshman, or they needed to fill their diversity quotas because I checked all of the boxes. Black, White, and Filipino. None of this mattered to me, because I knew that peoples' external negative energy was based in their own fears and failures. This goes directly with a quote by Criss Jami, an American poet that says, *"The hated man is the result of his hater's pride rather than his hater's conscience."* Other students who had internships congratulated me and we talked about our respective companies, but those who didn't get a call back or didn't do too well in their interview bombarded me with their critiques. I knew that nothing was going to knock me off my path and I was trailblazing the way for my brothers and the next set of freshmen so I couldn't fail. Shannon Alder said it best when he said, *"You will face your biggest opposition when you are closest to your biggest miracle."* Despite this realization of the behaviors of people, there were a couple people who stayed positive and in my corner throughout it all.

Kyle Broadnax was the student in a grade above me who I quickly aspired to be like when I got to campus. He was the current Treasurer of MBA, knew everyone on campus, had landed an internship as a freshman with the same company, and basically took me under his wing. Even as I am writing this, I could call Kyle right now and he would still gladly give me advice, talk about business, or go to the basketball gym right now and try and guard me. However, this is an important lesson because you always want to keep leveling up in life. Earlier I talked about how "iron sharpens iron" and I applied this methodology to our relationship, but I took it a step further with the quote of "Work until your idols become your rivals." Now that Kyle and I had been placed on somewhat of a level playing field, the strive I had to be just like him, turned into how I can competitively overcome my former mentor and advance myself further, whilst still remaining friends.

Another reason that the Lone Wolf Mentality came naturally

to me was because of the lack of black male representation in my environment. When Kyle and I went to our accepted offers banquet with the company, we were the only two black men in a room full of close to 50-60 people. Combine that with me being the only freshman in the room, I certainly turned a lot of heads and made a few enemies as well. The silver lining of the night was that we were able to bask in the financial bounty of interning with a large company. We received very nice clothing, water bottles, chargers, bags, and school supplies with the company's logo on it, which led to even more people calling me "extra" and narcissistic because I decided to wear and display something that I earned and worked extremely hard for.

The company also held a Signature Series workshop on campus, which essentially was a three-session workshop for freshman interested in the company to come and learn about the business, the industry, and to potentially apply for an internship the end of their sophomore year. There were about 12-15 people in the room who were all wanting to move forward with the company and who kept trying to get a "leg-up" on one another to impress the recruiters. When we all introduced ourselves, I sat in the back, and the introductions started from the front. Everyone said their name, where they were from, as well as something they were involved in. It started out with some people saying they were involved with nothing yet, others saying they had joined groups, and then some people said they had already started their own organizations.

When it came to me I calmly and simply said my name, hometown, and that I would be interning with the company in the summer in the Cincinnati region. That cut all the competitiveness out of the room, but instead of looking down upon my peers, I used this opportunity to help them with their resumes and interviewing skills so that they would be better equipped when they applied next year. There is a very big false step and misconception when you accomplish something, and you can tell who the people are that let power go to their heads. Instead of asserting my dominance in the room and coming in with my chest out like I was the golden boy, I decided to use my status to help others gain leverage and aid them in the same process that my mentors aided me. The National Association for Black Accountants detail their logo as "Lifting as We Climb" which truly resonates with me, and this goes back to our earlier discussion about success. A lot of people can have major individual success, but who are you also helping get to the next level, what is your legacy as a person? These are the questions we need to start asking ourselves because that is truly what comprises a better working world. When you start to build up others as you do yourself and instilling the same mission of giving back that you have lived by, pretty soon you are creating a supporting village (**LONE WOLF TIP #2**) that could possibly nurture the next successful or important person.

It always pays to be nice, no matter who you are or who you are talking too. It is funny how quickly situations can change, especially in business, and it is imperative that you also build a bridge and leave it intact. In the Spring semester, there is a slightly smaller career fair called Spring ICE, where companies look to secure more internships as they head into the summer employment season. There was a complete paradigm shift in how I interacted with the two fairs. In the Fall, I was handing out my resumes and business cards, dishing my elevator speeches out left and right, and patiently waiting my turn to speak with recruiters.

In the Spring career fair, I was invited on behalf of my company to help assist the recruiters, so I was taking people's resumes, listening to their elevator speeches, and aligning myself with the company's goals. Seniors and juniors would ask me how

long I have been with the company, and I would say I am interning with them and I am a freshman here at Miami. They thought
I meant grad school or something and they couldn't comprehend
that this freshman was taking their senior status resume on behalf
of the company they were looking to intern with.

These were the same people telling me a semester earlier that
companies aren't interested in freshman and internships are
mainly reserved for sophomores and juniors, and now you had
to go through me to get to this company. It just goes to show that
being nice to everyone has their benefits because you never know
who will be put in certain opportunities. When my freshman
friends came up to the booth super nervous and intimidated, I
would invite them over and go over their resume and elevator
pitch with them to calm their nerves down, as well as pass their
resume along to someone who I know would actually read it.
Never forget that people do business with who they know and
who they like.

Being with the company came with a lot of perks. I was flown
out to New York in January for the first time and put up in a
large, extravagant hotel for a company conference with around
200 of the future interns. I got to establish connections and meet
people across the nation who were thriving in their own states
and universities. I kept looking around and saw nothing but
young and determined leaders who all share my similar mindset.
The company made us go on a scavenger hunt in Grand Central
Station, I went on my first yacht and had a full course banquet,
and even traveled to Times Square. I was originally going to
stay in bed because it was snowing and freezing outside but my
friend, Aleigha Mason, convinced me to travel the streets of New
York City. I had to also make sure it was a priority of mine to
visit Carlo's Bakery because I was obsessed with Cake Boss, the
TV show about the bakery, for the longest. I ended the short

excursion with a parting bag full of company gear comprised of hats, scarves, gloves, notebooks, and a renewed excitement to start interning with the company.

The next large event was after freshman year ended, and I was flown out to New Jersey to have our national training. This was twice the size of the first function, because it was every intern in my program and my network grew even more. Kyle was flown out with me as well and we went through our extensive onboarding process. This consisted of getting our company bags, laptops, badges, company credit card, office layouts, and policy training. This process is what really made it feel official and I had fully understood the blessed situation I was in when I returned to Cincinnati and started working in the company building. When I got my first paycheck that was triple any job I had worked at before really made me catch my breath for a moment. It was the most money I had ever seen in my name at once and it had a comma on it. I felt like I was on top of the world. This was the beginning to a great summer internship.

Our office was in the heart of Cincinnati, right across from the Cincinnati Reds and Bengals stadium, overlooking the Ohio River. The company culture was hard-working, but very casual and laid back with a lot of the employees wearing jeans or khakis. I kept to my same mindset and came in with my suit on every single day, because I always knew that I had eyes on me.

. . . .

LONE WOLF TIP #5
Don't Get Comfortable

One major mistake that interns make is thinking that because they secured the internship and attended the conferences and trainings, they are set and done with working hard because they have "made it." They stop putting forth the maximum and intense effort it took to reach that position and feel like they have earned themselves a break. Every single millionaire and business guru will tell you that complacency is the enemy of progress. You put forth all of that effort and work to open the door of opportunity and walk through it, but now you must perform at an even higher level than what it took to get there. Always remember that business is dog-eat-dog and there is always someone coming for your position.

. . . .

During my internship, I was placed in an advisory and consulting role, which is where I fell in love with consulting. My client was one of the largest Fortune 500 multinational consumer goods companies in the world, and I conducted very high-level in-depth research on user experience and user interface portal design, with a focus on generational and millennial impact as a target consumer base. This means that I was doing research on what makes my generation, and the generation below me, interested and engaged in terms of mobile design interfaces and app layout. This was my first real entry into the consulting realm because I got to work with my client, listen to what they needed, and then worked with my team to come up with multiple viable solutions based upon weeks and weeks of insightful research. I wasn't just learning about things from a textbook, I was thrown into the fire and told to come up with the best solutions. There was a reason I was assigned that role and allowed the opportunity to work within it and be placed on other major projects simultaneously. It was because I made myself stand out in the office to the Senior Managers and Partners of the company.

Much like my Lone Wolf Method in college, I applied it to the internship experience as well. I showed up early before anyone even came to the office to get some extra work done, also because I was taking online Calculus at the same time. I showed initiative and became the spokesperson for Miami University's social media coverage on internships. While working at the company, I was able to demonstrate the company through various layers of Instagram. This rejuvenated the office because partners and senior managers loved to be able to be on the new growing trend of social media and explain what they do, while the younger members of the office felt comfortable in their conscious realm of experience with social media. I also went to lunch with a lot of the high-level partners and was able to learn a lot about their background and their contribution to the company.

Everything I just talked about now was very surface level of how business operates and how to be successful in those areas, but there are always multiple ways of doing business that isn't always marketed or talked about. Using your leverage within your network is extremely important during internships. The largest partner in my office happened to be a Miami alumnus, and he invited me to an important charity board meeting where there were multiple CEO's and influential people in the Cincinnati region. The partner also invited me in to listen in on a conference call of his. He was discussing the largest client he oversaw, and he was using hundreds of millions of dollars in plain conversation like it was nothing to him. True business is conducted in these intimate settings where everyone knows each other. The atmosphere is different, and true power radiates inside of the room.

The conclusion of your internship is arguably the most important part of the entire program. They are looking at you to see how you can conclude yourself in a professional way, while maintaining your presence and not be forgotten. Most people send "thank you emails" as part of their departure from the internship, which are very good and help to leave a nice impression. But I understand people's behaviors and understand that the act of receiving something physical goes a long way. I emailed everyone at the conclusion of my internship, as well as wrote personal cards to every partner, senior manager, and manager who I worked with. The recipients responded to me with more enthusiasm and gratitude than compared to the emails. You also want to leave more excited about the future opportunity than before you even started. Lastly, stay in touch with who worked on your team, or people you met in the office, because you never know who could rise or leave in the time that you are gone.

Chapter Recap

KEY IDEAS

1. Don't let people's perceptions of reality project on to you. Do what they say was impossible, venture where they said was impassable, and strive for what they were too scared to do.

2. Knowing this, you're going to have a lot of critics and haters in everything you do. That just means you are doing something right.

3. Never get complacent, no matter how much success you attain. The moment you stop working hard is the moment you become vulnerable.

REFLECTION QUESTIONS

1. When is one time you defied the odds or went outside the box of societal normality? How did others react around you?

2. Have you ever felt like your role or position was threatened? Or did you ever usurp someone and take their place?

3. Have you ever interned before? If not, what are some steps you can take to ensure you stand out during the whole process?

4. Who and what does your network consist of right now?

LONE WOLF TIP #5: **Don't Get Comfortable**

CHAPTER 5

Ascent

To anyone looking at my position from the outside, they would think I had my life secured and could sit back and reap the benefits of all my hard work. However, I still was hungry for more success. It was like an insatiable beast that could never be quenched. This is not to be confused with a lack of content or lust for greed and wealth, I just knew that there were more opportunities out there that I was slowly becoming more and more ready for. This opportunity presented itself at a networking event right before my internship started, and it came through the social media platform LinkedIn.

. . . .

LONE WOLF TIP #6
Use Social Media To Your Advantage

Leverage social media to your benefit, and make sure you are utilizing it to its full potential. Often, we think of social media as photo sharing applications, quick messaging platforms, or only status updates on your life. There is so much societal nonsense on social media that clouds a lot of positive things the platform can do. You have control over who you follow and what you look at, so start making changes to follow things that coexist with your passion. If you are into photography, follow pages and people in that field that can help you network in that industry, or give you ideas on how to better your own craft. If you are into business, then start looking and connecting with other entrepreneurs and innovators such as Gary Vaynerchuk, who is the CEO of VaynerMedia, and a popular name in the entrepreneurial realm. Your mindset starts to shift from trying to find the "hottest" girl or guy near you, to actively upgrading a skill or passion you have, and investing in your own source of knowledge. Just as how your body is a machine that runs off what you put inside, like fruits & vegetables, your mind is also cognizant of what you're putting inside of it. Understand that if you excessively fill your mind with pornography, negativity, hatred, and other people's social media, then that is what your mind is going to consist of. Feed your mind the same energy and food you fill your healthy body such as podcasts, self-help books, or attending conferences and workshops about your interests. It is also very helpful to have a LinkedIn page, which essentially is a professional social media platform that lets you network and connect with other business people around the world, and in your field.

. . . .

One month after I had finished my first year at Miami, I was bombarded with LinkedIn messages about this event called Black Achievers, which was an event that brought a lot of business professionals in the African-American community under one place to network and share stories. I originally brushed it off as nothing of my concern, but decided to go because it was free, close to my house, and my friend Kenny Glenn decided to go as well. I decided to take my own advice and step out of my comfort zone, which led to me being in the right room at the right time, with the right people. Patrick Overton, an American author, verbalizes this idea best when he says *"When you walk to the edge of all the light you have and take that first step into the darkness of the unknown, you must believe that one of two things will happen. There will be something solid for you to stand upon or you will be taught to fly."*

When we walked into this very nice hotel, we were taken

aback when we realized that we were the youngest people in the entire program. There were business owners, employees, entrepreneurs at this event, so my business cards really came in handy that night. It was great to network with people of color in the business workforce, but I just kept saying how this was a waste of my time and I was about to leave, Kenny made me stay for the last Keynote Speaker because he had heard that he was doing big things in the area. So grumpily, I stayed, and this man walks up to the podium who carried himself with the subtle confidence of a businessman, quieted everyone down, and started speaking. He instantly commanded the room and even people from outside of the event poked their heads into the ballroom to see who was speaking with such a strong and powerful tone.

This man's name was J.C. Baker, and he spoke about the illusion of black billionaires and how we don't understand what real money is, but we will point to Robert Smith, Michael Jordan, and Oprah as the zenith of black financial success. He exclaimed that all three net worth's of these individuals combined was still "monopoly money" compared to the major business people in the world. Then he went on to talk about how his consulting firm was doing work with the NBA, NFL, Google, and other large companies, and I am sitting there with my jaw unhinged thinking "I really NEED to connect with him, because he is talking about all of the things in my head, but on a grandeur scale."

After his extremely compelling speech and presentation, I approached him and introduced myself and said I wanted to learn more about what you do and learn as early as I could. When I told him I was 19, he slightly raised his eyes and told me to come to his office sometime and we could talk. Without missing a beat, I said, "I will be there tomorrow just tell me what time." On the drive home I called my parents and told them that I had a feeling something major was going to happen because of that networking event, and they said that the Lord works in mysterious ways.

I showed up at his office the next day in my nicest suit and my notebook in hand ready to learn all I could. He said I was not the average 19-year-old and had me sign a couple non-disclosure forms because he was going to allow me to sit in on his first client for the day. We walked into the conference room and there was an ex-NFL player who wanted to create a business because he told me that the NFL stood for Not-For-Long, and that professional athletes need to learn business so they don't get taken advantage of and become broke within a couple of years. According to Sports Illustrated, 80% of NFL athletes go broke within two years of retirement, and 60% of NBA players go bankrupt within five years.

I got to sit down beside him and listen to J.C. explain what the company was, and even I wasn't ready for what was about to happen. Essentially, J.C. Baker & Associates is a comprehensive consulting firm that specializes in the optimization and growth of businesses. The clientele of the company ranges from single individuals, startups, and new businesses, all the way towards major Fortune 500 companies. There was a company jet, clients as far as Germany and Australia, and companies invested in tech, renewable energy, restaurant, and even retail. My mind was blown more than it had been already.

I brought some other people from my inner circle to J.C.'s office because I wanted to reach back and pull those who supported me on this journey as well. I brought Kyle, Kenny, and Roderick Mills who is now playing professional ball overseas and has an amazing blog called the Relentless Finisher. This is what spearheaded the creation of the Junior Consultant branch of the company. We were now responsible for client acquisition, project management, and front-line communications. The involvement was different than my internship because I was seeing all the behind the scenes involvement of how business really worked and was able to do work at a level that an intern at other big companies would never be able to see or do. J.C. became my mentor in the business realm, from learning about credit, to different industries, to sales, and consulting.

· ·

LONE WOLF TIP #7
Mentors Expedite Success

Mentors are one of the keys to success. Every successful person has someone who has shown them some type of way because it reduces risk and failure and provides trusted guidance from a path that has been proven true. I implore you to be very cautious with everyone who calls themselves a mentor, and the screening process is very simple. If someone calls themselves a "mentor" or "personal life coach" and are asking for money in exchange for their services, then they are probably not legit. You'll know when you have found someone who has taken you under their wing when the results speak for themselves and you can feel yourself learning and bettering yourself. Through J.C. I started really understanding business, how to manage clients and sales teams that worked under me, and how to truly conduct the business of consulting.

· ·

I quickly rose in favor over the other Junior Consultants after my summer internship because I sacrificed and displayed my dedication and willingness to learn while being in school at the same time. I would ask to be on all the conference calls, travel to meetings and events, and bring my own clients to J.C. I would literally leave an accounting lecture at school, and then hop on a client call with J.C. about the very thing we were talking about in class. It was direct application of learning concepts to real world material, to which I was a direct beneficiary of, and this expedited my learning. I became the Lone Wolf businessman that I aspired to be because I MADE it come true in the ENVIRONMENT I placed myself in. Don't wait for anyone to tell you when it is your time or place to be great, go seek it yourself and claim it outright while waiting for nobody.

. . . .

LONE WOLF TIP #8
Stop TALKING and Start DOING

People have amazing ideas every day and they think it is the next million-dollar idea. Whether it is an app, a business, or a new invention or concept, it doesn't matter unless there is dedicated application. It doesn't matter what is in your head unless you use your hands, which means do the work. For example, if you want to be a doctor, then you can read all the books you want and watch all the videos. But unless you go to school, both undergraduate and medical, and shadow real doctors hands-on through internships and completing your residency, you won't become a certified doctor.

. . . .

J.C. placed me in charge of Nexgen Vapors, which is a vapor shop distribution center headquartered in Dayton, Ohio. I had to build a sales team and train them to push our FDA compliant product into vapor shops nationwide. Through this project I learned about sales and marketing, legal implications, social context and how it influences business, how to manage a sales team across the nation, and I learned greatly about the Food & Drug industry and administration. These are skills that you just can't learn all in a classroom, and I was learning them at an exponential rate. I remember sitting in class while the teacher was instructing us on cost of goods sold, and I was l literally moving product from my phone and laptop across the entire country.

I also oversaw helping our clients out when they came and sold their product at Miami University. During football season, one of our clients who has a business selling their product called the Alum Clock, which are fully patented granite clocks, came up to Miami and I was able to introduce them to the President of the university because of my connections and status.

Working with J.C. made my focus even more honed in on what I wanted to accomplish in life because I could see where my future was heading. I wasn't a W-2 employee with the company so everything I did was purely in the name of entrepreneurship and gaining as much knowledge and experience I could. I did manage to receive a free professional photoshoot with the company because a member of our firm, Chris Stets, has a professional personal studio in his background. He is the Chief Marketing Officer of our company and he is a major reason the movie Terminator came to life, as well as work on the branding for Girl Scouts of America.

I started to understand the value of what I brought to the company from a perspective of my age and my generation. We had a potential E-Sports client who was brought into the office and J.C. had no idea what E-Sports was and what that realm consisted of. Leaning on my background in gaming and knowledge in League of Legends and other E-Sports, I was able to be a liaison between the client and J.C. in explaining the ins and outs of the industry. When Aaron Ryan, who is a high executive in the NBA 2K League and Miami alumnus, came to visit I was able to talk to him on a professional level above just a student panel, and it was opportunities like this where I was able to continue standing out and shining above those around me.

The most important lesson I learned, was what failure looked like and how to become accustomed to it. When I first started Nexgen Vapors, it was just me and my brother Drew going around to the stores who wouldn't pay us any piece of mind. We went from store to store with rejection looming behind us, growing darker in the distance, and it seemed like with every step forward we were taking two steps back. Similar to when I would try and find clients to bring to J.C. and get on the phone with them, they would either turn down working with me, nobody would answer back, or I would get far in the client relationship process only to have them back out at the last minute during the financing proposal stage. That is why I understand that the path of an entrepreneur is a long and tedious one, with strenuous ups and downs, and no form of consistency. So, to everyone who wants to call themselves and entrepreneur, or delve into that space, be very cautious that your mental fortitude must be impenetrable because it is a very hard life.

Earlier when I talked about sacrifice, I truly meant that there were some things I realized I had to give up in order to be great. I started staying in during weekends to conduct industry research, and work on my clients and the business. I had to drive from my campus to the office with a minimal amount of income coming in, on top of being a "broke college student," so I could engage in client meetings or be able to be taught more business lessons from J.C. I also had to do this by myself, which led to a deeper understanding of the Lone Wolf. Even the colleagues I brought to J.C. when I originally went to his office started showing up less and less for their own personal reasons and becoming less engaged. I showed up by myself to meetings before and after classes, handled a lot of the grunt work for the company by myself, and inserted myself in meetings where I thought I should be. The other Junior Consultants would engage a little from time to time, but I was on the ground floor showing my dedication and aspirations to be greater than what I currently was, which is why I became the most trusted and standout Junior Consultant.

Even during winter break when everyone studies abroad, works to generate more income, or take vacations in more warmer climates, I was sacrificing and grinding with J.C.

I started to take more charge in finding my own clients, really listening to their problems, and implementing facets of the company to demonstrate our expertise and proficiency in the areas that the client was lacking in. This really started to strengthen my consulting skills. I became more involved in the company and learned just how vast the vault of knowledge and the types of global connections we had: From learning about the entire process of buying a car, to understanding credit and a basic foundational understanding of Forex & Stock Market Trading, to Real Estate, how a Minority Business Enterprise Structure works, and the hotbed of new tech companies. In actuality, I was taking a conglomeration of business courses, I just wasn't paying an atrocious amount of money for knowledge like I did in the college system. I even got to experience doing business with a lot of high-profile people, which would have never happened in school. I'll never forget when J.C. sent me a message saying there was a very high chance he was about to be in a meeting with Shaq and Tiger Woods, and then proceed to get on the phone with people from Lil Wayne's record label to provide music for our patented project called Pro Elite Training.

For all my budding entrepreneurs and young business professionals, I would like to impart some knowledge about the fundamentals of sales, the six secrets to persuasion, and the five powerful motivators of people. These are examples of what I mean when I explained that I was learning business at an accelerated rate being involved in actual sales and client work, then just learning about it in the classroom. The Three C's of Sales, along with the other examples, is one of the first foundational methods to business that J.C. taught me, and this understanding of people and sales is what gave me the skills to lead a national sales team.

The Three C's of Sales

Understanding the Three C's of Sales is extremely important and transcendent across any industry. Whether you are looking to go into real estate, consulting, pharmaceuticals, tech, or the food and beverage industry, you must understand how sales are conducted and people's behaviors surrounding them.

- **Cash:** People pay with actual dollars, which has proven to be a more emotional transaction, because they are physically handing over money. Usually you pay a slightly lesser price of the overall ticket, because you do not have to finance the purchase, i.e. a car purchase.

- **Credit:** People either have remotely good credit, or remotely bad credit. Credit is based on a range from 300-900, with around 620 being the average score that is viable to make purchases with. People with good credit tend to be more ungrateful about their purchases because they know that they can qualify for just about anything. People with bad credit tend to more thankful for the transactions because they know they need something and have a lower chance of qualifying for it.

- **Collateral:** This is something that people usually put up when they don't have cash or good enough credit. An example would be putting your house or car up for collateral, and if you don't make your payments on time or in the full amount, the person who loaned you the transaction that you received is entitled to repossess what you put up for collateral.

The Six Secrets of Persuasion

These insights into people's behaviors were passed down to me by Dr. J.C. Baker, and were originally founded by Dr. Robert Cialdini. These secrets of persuasion can be very useful with implementation of your sales and marketing strategies and having a holistic understanding of what a layer of business looks like.

- **Consensus**: This is using societal norms to persuade people. Saying that because everyone else likes or does it, I should be doing it too.

- **Consistency**: Consistent behavior, a clean and positive track record, and loyalty are factors that help companies stay in business and convince their customers or clients to continue utilizing their services.

- **Authority**: You are more likely to listen to someone who is an expert or a proven leader in their fields. People will listen to J.C.Baker because he had been doing consulting and sales for over twenty years, but a lot more people will listen to Dr. Baker because his Doctorate in Leadership speaks for itself.

- **Reciprocity**: This is doing something for someone before they even ask about it. When you go out on a limb and provide an aspect of your service, or do a great job without someone telling you, then they are more likely to fully do more business with you.

- **Liking**: People do business with who they like and people stray leagues away from people they don't like. If someone doesn't like you or your business, then they are prone to telling other people negative things about your business. First impressions count!

- **Scarcity**: Lines like "While supplies last" or "Limited Time Offer" persuade people to buy and influence their time and decision-making skills.

The Five Powerful Motivators of People

If you want to start a company, are currently running a company, or want to know what drives people, then these are the top five motivators for people. Whether they are older adults, millennials, or even generations to come, these core principles will stay the same in terms of their relevance.

- **Money:** Money actually is one of the least primary motivators compared to the four other motivators. You could be making six figures in a job and hate coming to work every single day, which is little to no motivation if not a negative amount.

- **Autonomy:** People want to feel like they aren't just puppets on a string doing the same repetitive task over and over. They want variety in their work to stay motivated, so they don't feel like they are programmed robots.

- **Mastery:** People have a desire to be great. That is why we watch cooking shows, pro athletes, and admire the top entrepreneurs, because people innately want to better themselves and master a skill.

- **Purpose:** If someone is employed in a company, they want to feel like whatever work they are doing matters to the company. If they do not feel like they are making a change, then they feel inadequate to the people around them and become less motivated at their task.

- **Meaning:** This is arguably the most important motivator for people. What is the mission of the company they are at, or the work that they are doing? Are they buying into the communication of the long-term vision and invested into the people who are leading them? These are questions that employees and employers need to ask themselves if they want to motivate people.

Because of my involvement with J.C. and accompanying him on the numerous meetings and client conference he went to, I started meeting a lot of millionaires. One of our partners that I work directly with is a multi-millionaire, and we are creating a company based in the water remediation industry. I remember him telling a family story and he mentioned a large house in front of a nice pool that was beside the basketball court, adjacent to the pool house. And I thought to myself, one day I'll get out of the dorm life and be able to buy my parents a house like that or even bigger. There were multiple clients and partners of ours who were doctors and attorneys, business owners, celebrities, and smart investors who all were completely secure in their finances and regarded highly in their fields. The only thing that caught me off guard, was that I never knew they were millionaires until I was told by J.C. after. I learned one of the most important wealth lessons from these various meetings.

. . . .

LONE WOLF TIP #9
The Goal is to Be Rich, Not Look Rich

A lot of rich and wealthy people are some of the most plain-looking human beings you will ever see. Most of the time you won't even know if a millionaire is rich or not, because they have nothing to prove. They aren't buying the newest cars, expensive clothes, and trying to parade their wealth through external means. Jeff Bezos was still driving his old Toyota Camry he originally bought, even though his own personal net worth had just surpassed a billion dollars. Mark Zuckerberg wears the same outfit every day to reduce decision time in picking out clothes in the morning, and it is not an outfit filled with designer logos and name brands, just an ordinary plain outfit. Use common sense with your money. Don't buy a $500 designer bag to have $75 in it. These **LONE WOLF TIPS** are garnered from those who know what real money and success looks like. Don't believe everything by just viewing it from a surface level. I started learning how to save to invest and educating those around me with financial literacy and money managing tips because it was about my own personal legacy, and who can I bring with me on this journey to success and generational wealth. Pop culture and what is trending in the mainstream is not reality.

. . . .

Chapter Recap

KEY IDEAS

1. Turn your mind into an impenetrable fortress and be the personal gatekeeper to choose what exactly goes in.

2. Feed your mind the same healthy foods and content that you would feed your body, or else you will be mentally sluggish and weak.

3. Greatness is a sacrifice, if you aren't prepared to give it your all then you will be surpassed by somebody who wants it more than you.

REFLECTION QUESTIONS

1. Who are some mentors in your life that can help you develop? If you don't have any, then how can you seek those mentors out now?

2. What are your thoughts about buying super expensive things? Do you think that objects alone determine your wealth and success?

3. How can you push yourself outside of your comfort zone, and in which areas? Will doing this help you to conquer your weaknesses?

4. Think about the environment you are currently in. Is this environment conducive to what you want to accomplish in life and become successful in completing your goals? What environment should you be in to maximize the potential inside of you?

LONE WOLF TIP #6: **Use Social Media To Your Advantage**

LONE WOLF TIP #7: **Mentors Expedite Success**

LONE WOLF TIP #8: **Stop TALKING and Start DOING**

LONE WOLF TIP #9: **The Goal is to Be Rich, Not Look Rich**

CHAPTER 6
Quotidian Balance

According to Merriam-Webster, the word "quotidian" means to occur every single day. This chapter we will be discussing and taking an in-depth look at what the day-to-day habits are of successful people. The Spectrem Group ran a composite study and survey and concluded, in their market insight report, that there were close to 11 million millionaires in the United States as of 2018. Not every single person has the same exact schedule, method to success, and habitual lifestyle, but they all collectively share about the same patterns of quotidian balance that the wealthy abide by. We are going to see exactly what these tangible methods are, while learning the process of instilling these same habits into our everyday lives. Remember, it takes 21 days to build a habit, and 90 days to build a lifestyle.

Business and life can be unpredictable, chaotic, and sometimes too much to handle in certain points in our lives. However, we must always keep a positive attitude and focus on the things that we can control. Think about what could be the very first productive thing that you can do right after you open your eyes in the morning. If you answered with "making your bed" then you are on the right track and I will see you striving alongside me on the path to success. Making your bed every morning is crucial to success in terms of discipline and control, and it is the very first thing I do when I get out of bed, followed by my morning pushups. This allows me to start my morning with a clear head and know that in the midst of the chaotic twists and turns throughout the day, I will be returning to a bed that I made myself. It also gives you a sense of satisfaction, because even before you really got started with your day, you have already set your mind to completing tasks. This is standard practice from those in the armed forces, and it instills a sense of discipline in yourself and sets the tone for not only the entire day, but the rest of the week, and then the month. Then when you look back at all the years you got up and made your bed in the morning, you have unconsciously trained yourself to handle no excuses, and to not do things half-heartedly. You understand to do things and complete tasks with the best of your ability because you know, that just like the bed that YOU made and YOU have to sleep in later, all of your work is a reflection of YOU.

In college, the myth is that noodles and pizza are the only things that are accessible to eat, and that you will gain the "freshman fifteen" weight gain during your first year. These myths become true for the people who actually go through with following that regiment and adding drinking and little physical energy on top of that and the weight gain is more like a "terrible twenty." Earlier I talked about how your body is a temple, and reacts to what you put inside of it, and this is very accurate when you start to analyze people's eating habits. It is important to not only instill habitual times to eat throughout the day, but also make an effort to eat healthy here and there so you are not just filling your body with junk and trash that slow you down and make you feel sluggish.

A lot of people find themselves to be too busy to eat or they forget meals throughout the day, but I always think of my eating time in two parts. One is to fuel my body with the right foods to prepare for whatever comes next, whether that is working out, going to class, or even preparing for sleep because it is not wise to eat a whole pizza and then go straight to sleep. The second part is that I consolidate my time of relaxation and recuperation within my eating breaks. Some people complain they don't have time in the day but will spend hours binge-watching Netflix shows, which doubly takes away from key study or working time. I believe in a self-created Fixed Time Principle, where we can personally control the construct of our reality of time by how we engage with ourselves throughout the day. Have you ever just been lying in bed and started scrolling on social media or playing a video game, and then you look up and hours have passed by without you knowing "where the time went?" This is because you are not planning your breaks out and not having a realistic grip on time. When you plan out to eat for a certain period while you are on social media or catching up on a show, then you have satisfied both your hunger, and your personal appeasement, all while controlling the amount of time that you allotted yourself to have. This is very important with busy college schedules, and career schedules, because just as the famous saying goes, time is money.

Once you start instilling your eating habits, you can then have enough fuel and focus to put towards your daily physical activity. You don't have to be a gym fanatic, or a collegiate and professional athlete to stay in shape, and this is something that a vast majority of successful people say that they do every day. Incorporating some type of physical workout or activity into your day helps relieve stress, gives you a personal challenge, and a greater sense of accomplishment upon completion of your goal. I am an avid visitor of my local recreational center, where I play basketball and go into the gym where I can challenge myself with new weights, workouts, and rivals every single day. I also apply the Fixed Time Principle here because I personally believe that you don't need to spend hours at the gym, in fact, I think the longer you stay the more detrimental it is to your goal. Think about what people normally do at the gym. They come in and take a while to warm up and choose their machines or workouts, then they are on their phones or talking to other people most of the time, and then they allow themselves multiple long breaks in between their sets. Cut out all the excessive distractions and come in with a keen focus on what you are going to do, how you are going to do it, and take minimal breaks to maximize the effort of your workout. Now, not only are you competing against yourself and the weights and workouts you choose, you are also competing against a self-imposed time limit. Personally, if I am at the gym for more than 75 minutes, I am wasting time and not appropriating my attention to the task at hand. That is why if you ever catch me in the gym, you will probably think I am the most pissed off person in the world, but in reality, I just got my headphones in and block everything out and focus on myself. I know what workout I am doing for the day, you might be a genuine person, but if you are intruding into my personal time that I allotted to better myself, I view you as a threat and a distraction.

The next quotidian habit you want to start building is one that is personal and is a passion or stress reliever. Find. A. Hobby. You may already have one, but finding a hobby is different than leisure time watching TV or playing games. This is the time where you can actively train yourself in a skill you want to learn, or pursue something that you have genuine interest in. For me, I have a huge interest and passion in music because I have been playing the piano for years, was in my school's jazz band, and I love to sing, so this is my hobby that I invest time in because it means a lot to me. I allow myself that time in between classes and assignments to stretch my creative muscles, because I feel at peace and in control when I am writing music and singing my old-school R&B jams on the piano. Whether your craft is writing poetry, drawing and painting, coding, skateboarding, reading, or even cooking, find your avocation in your life and actively cultivate it within your day or week.

When we are talking about millionaires and their successful habits, I like to start with close to the top of the list. Billionaire Warren Buffett is one of the wealthiest persons in the entire world. He is an investment guru, a business mogul, and a famous public speaker. He, and many other wealthy and successful people, agree that reading is essential to their continuous vault of knowledge. Reading sharpens your mind, lets you learn new skills or traits, uncover somebody's life story, and helps you to understand the world. It is said that Buffet reads around 500 pages a day, and if you want to put this in financial terms, he regards knowledge from reading books as compound interest. The more books you read and knowledge you accumulate, the higher your wisdom and intellect grows upon itself. Start reading about the industry you want to go into or important people who you look up too and follow their accounts of what made them successful. If you want to go into business, read the Economist, Wall Street Journal, and Forbes to increase your business acumen in the field, and the same goes for any other industry.

. . . .

LONE WOLF TIP #10
Pursue Knowledge

Knowledge is one the most important tools a person can have because it can't physically be taken away once you have studied and learned the subject or material. Start actively pursuing knowledge because it is the only way to start compounding that interest in terms of wisdom and intellect. Substitute social media and You-Tube at night for reading at least an hour before you go to bed. Exchange Netflix and Hulu for Ted Talks and webinars that shed light on what you want to learn about. Instead of listening to the newest album that came out by "Lil' Whatever" start purposefully listening to podcasts that are held by people you admire in your field. You need to truly understand that you are NEVER done learning. Professors at the highest academic level are still students, professional athletes who are All-Stars in their position are still training, musicians who have won Grammys and other awards are still practicing their scales. You can become like them by adding a routine book that you read daily that allows you to not only build the intellect in the area you want, but also allows you to focus on yourself and disconnect from an overly excessive digital age.

. . . .

You need to start keeping a daily journal of your experiences. This helps me to compile multiple transcripts of nostalgia, and to authentically reflect on what happened that day, week, or month. A lot of successful people have a journal or calendar that they write everything down in and write their future goals in. You are conversing with yourself in the present and discussing yourself in the future. That is why I said earlier in the book that you must become your own best friend. When you are able to have very high-level conversations with yourself, you'll be able to start seeing the bigger picture of things and start to play in the long-term game. It also helps to write down what you are thankful for, and what you have been blessed with to make sure that you are always kept grounded and stable.

Understand that someone always has it better, and worse than you, but all we need to focus on is our own personal form of success. An example of this would be about how the hypothetical second richest person in the world was on his yacht envying the richest man in the world who was flying above him in his jet, while the third richest person in his luxury car wishes he could one day own a boat. While all this is going on, the person waiting for the bus stop wishes that he could one day have a car, and the person who he is envied by is someone who has to walk everywhere because he can't afford a bus ticket. Now you would think that the person who is walking is at the nethermost position in this example, but the man who is in the wheelchair looking from his window quietly wishes that he could walk like the man outside. This example just serves to prove that there is always someone above and beneath you, and that a major form of success is personal contentment and happiness.

Moving forward, the next habit of successful people is that most wealthy people have a system or process to handle their organizational strategy that they abide by. Everyone works in different ways. Some people like writing things down in a calendar, having an assistant tell them where to go, or by just memorizing everything for the day. You would be surprised about how many people with photographic memories I have encountered, with J.C. being one of them. For me personally, I take every Sunday to prepare for the week and outline how my days are going to look. I physically write down what assignments are due, important dates and meetings, and client calls, on a checklist that hangs on my wall. I find personal satisfaction in crossing things off myself when I complete them. Being organized will help you to prioritize things in your hectic schedule, which is an essential component of time management whether you are in high school, college, or well into your young adulthood years. You will be able to accurately implement time for the gym, or your hobby or passion, when you are fully organized because you will have that period allotted based on your priorities and can structure things around what is most important to you.

The last successful tip I want to impart on you is this concept of meditation. Meditation is something that my generation does not take advantage of, and really utilize to its fullest extent. Whether it is coupled with stretching and yoga or is just within the confines of your own personal stress, meditating helps you to become at peace with yourself and is the foundation for all of the other success tips. The best part about meditating is that you can think about whatever you want because it is YOUR head. You can think about what books you want to read, what hobby you want to practice next, what your upcoming week looks like, or where you see yourself in the future. In the mornings after you make your bed, or after you finish your hour session of reading right before you go to sleep, just take five or ten minutes to meditate and fully relax and discuss with yourself. The only lasting question that I will directly force you to ask yourself every night is "Are you getting better with each passing day? Does tomorrow allow me a chance to improve upon where I struggle, and if so, how can I tangibly make that happen?"

I implore you to research more success tips from other sources and dive deeper into the daily habits of wealthy people, but you will find that at least 90% of them have the same core principles that I listed here in this chapter. Once you start incorporating some of these basic doctrines into your life you will start to see a shift in your daily regiment, your physical and mental health, and your outlook on life. Coming from my own personal list of quotes "Tips are Habits that are just awaiting the process of implementation." So, I can give you all the tips that successful people do in your own personal lifestyle, but unless you follow **LONE WOLF TIP #8** and do the work, this will all be advice that will be dust in the wind. If you want to be successful, you must start training your mind and body to where success doesn't become just a goal, it becomes a habit of second nature. Your mornings set the framework for success, throughout the day you are actively going through the steps to be successful, and your evenings allow you the time for self-reflection on how you can be even more successful for the next day. Whether you are spiritual or not, this is the exact framework of the Lone Wolf Method based in Genesis 49:27.

Lastly, success is an actual word that you need to actively be incorporating into your daily vernacular. Shift your mindset to start being very selective of the words that you use, because your personal armory of your vocabulary provides the outlet of personification for your internal success. Instead of using the words "When I," "Maybe," "Soon," and "If," use words and phrases like "Now," "I Will," "This is How," and "I am Going to." Once you start making that transition step in your terminology, you will have taken the first steps to claiming success. You started by writing it down physically, then speaking it verbally, so the only thing left to do is actually Do The Work, to complete the Holy Trinity of Success.

Chapter Recap

KEY IDEAS

1. Create habits that turn into lifestyles. The most successful people have habits that are completed every single day as routines.

2. Discipline yourself by doing things to the fullest extent every single time and know that your first impression is reflected in your work.

3. Start verbalizing success and celebrating the "small wins" in life. Remember to be your own best friend and personal cheerleader.

REFLECTION QUESTIONS

1. What is this first thing you do when you open your eyes in the morning? Is this productive enough to be counted as a completed task?

2. What are some ways that you can seek out knowledge and actively learn?

3. How do you organize your life and your work? Are you someone who writes things down, set reminders in your phone, or just remember them in your head?

4. Meditate and think of the words that you use the most. Are you actively incorporating success into your vocabulary?

LONE WOLF TIP #10: Pursue Knowledge

CHAPTER 7

Young Money

Sooner or later you are going to have to take the financial training wheels off that your parents or supporters have bestowed upon you. Whether you are getting your first job in high school to save up for a car, working to put yourself through college, or are paying rent and living completely on your own for the first time, you need to understand how to manage your money. The harsh reality of the world is that nobody cares why you are behind on payments, or why you don't have enough money to pay for textbooks or can't afford to accommodate your personal lifestyle. When conversations turn down the convoluted path of "money," it can be very stressful and worrisome if you don't have a tight grip on your finances. Understand that money by itself is not right or wrong, but the way that it is distributed in the hands of the user are what determines that decision.

Gary Vaynerchuk, who is a serial entrepreneur and investor, talks about the subject of children and their parents a lot in his podcasts that concern money. Essentially, what he says is that if you are over the age of 22, and still complaining about your parent's lack of support financially, you have your priorities completely wrong. It is time for us to be financially literate, be able to handle our own accounts, and the earlier you learn these skills the better. I am not a finance guru, or investment wizard yet, but I do understand the basic concepts of money, especially when it comes to the lack of that area in our generation.

. . . .

LONE WOLF TIP #11
Understand Your Money

There are a lot of young adults and students at my school who party nearly every week and like to purchase food with their friends. Nothing is wrong with that, but the problem is the way in which they are doing it financially. My colleagues and peers will swipe their cards and hope they have enough money to cover it, and then never check their bank account balances for days and sometimes weeks. We have to learn how to audit our accounts. This a term that you probably hear your parents or financial advisors use a lot, but it simply means to internally review your receipts on what you have been purchasing. I check my bank account balance every other day, if not every day as one of my quotidian habits. Every month, your bank should send you a ledger or history of all the purchases you made during that time period, and you can see where the money is coming in from and to what categories or entities it is leaving towards. Whether that is food and drinks, bar covers, clothing, you have to see where your money is going and budget yourself accordingly based upon the amount of money you have coming in. This is a quick tip but people, even grown adults, still don't understand: If you are spending more money than you have coming in on a regular basis, then you are negatively impacting your account and are on the fast track to debt.

. . . .

To go along with the previous **LONE WOLF TIP**, you have to understand your own personal psychology towards money. Are you more swayed to spending food when all your friends are? Do you find yourself buying new articles of clothing every couple of weeks and then rarely wearing them? Do you really need these items and expenses, or are you just giving into societal peer pressure? This type of peer pressure comes with an actual cost too, so you have to be wary of how you are spending money and not hemorrhaging your bank accounts. Just as how we talked about having a focus and a purpose in the previous chapters, you must have financial goals set in order to instill some type of "dollar discipline." My goal is to pay off all my parent's debt, mortgages, and to make sure my brothers have a secure route to college so that the Phillips Empire will never have to worry about money troubles ever again. For some people it is saving up for a house or a car, or paying off your student loans, or getting ready to propose to the love of your life. Whatever it is, you have to have a plan financially.

Here is a quick financial example of the cost of going out on the weekends at my college.

Bar Cover $6
Drinks . . . . . $5-$15
Food $10
Transportation . . $7
—————————————
Total $28

This was a very modest estimate based off of my personal experiences and those of my friends in college. Sometimes people will buy $40 worth of drinks and go to two or three different bars in one night, but we will just say that the minimum for one weekend is $28. Most people go out Friday and Saturday, so the $28 becomes $56, and let's say they go out two weekends every month. So, going out and "partying" really is a $112 monthly expense, and people are having too much fun and praising "You Only Live Once" while they are bleeding out of their bank accounts and wondering why they are so broke. This example was at a very small-priced college town, but if you attend colleges in major cities and metropolitan areas, you could possibly see an increase of up to double the amount listed for each of those items on my hypothetical outing. A large aspect of the Lone Wolf Method is the financial freedom to not conform to the latest clothing styles and trends or having the "Fear Of Missing Out" (FOMO), which I hear a lot of college students complain about. They were forced to go out and really want to just go home. So you are SPENDING MONEY to think about BEING HOME. Was this because someone "forced" you to come out, or because your mental fortress wasn't strong enough to say no and wisely save your money?

Once you start learning about the basic principles of money by reading books about these topics, Dave Ramsey financial books are an excellent read, then you will start to feel more at peace financially. You won't have to always worry about if you have enough money, because you will start to learn how to not be accustomed to debt. Debt is not something to be normalized. Just because your parents have debt, or your friends have loans on top of loans to pay off their degree, doesn't mean that you have too as well. Don't take out thousands, or tens of thousands, out for student loans and then just say that you will develop a plan later and pay them off. One of the biggest mistakes I see people in high school and in college is that once they get comfortable, they stop looking for scholarships or putting money aside to plan for their student loans. Every penny matters. You might disagree with me, but I believe that at least taking a mental stand against your debt, will keep you from drowning in it.

It is very important to understand they types of loans you are taking out, from what companies you are getting the loan from, and what the respective interest rates are. That is up to your discretion to look and see your personal type of loans, but I will cover the difference between subsidized and unsubsidized loans. The major difference between these two loans, is that in the subsidized loan, the federal government will pay the interest for the time that the student is in college, or the loan has been qualified for a deferment. The unsubsidized loans are loans that begin accruing interest immediately once the loan has been taken out. Understanding the difference between these two entities will help you in making decisions on what type of loan you should try and take out. Obviously, a lot of these decisions are made by the college you are attending and are based off the numbers in your FASFA, the financial document you and your parents fill out to qualify for financial aid, but having that knowledge of the system at even a basic level will be very beneficial.

"Come open a credit card with my bank! There are a lot of perks for students and you want to build that credit early!" Warning. Stay away from these types of credit card sharks. When you turn 18, or even walk onto your college campus, there will be people trying to shove credit cards in your face nonstop. They prey on the new generation of debtors who they know are taking the beginning steps of financial independence and are coupled with the volatile spending tendencies of a teenage mindset. I personally recommend not even having an active credit card. Some people say that it is the main source of relief for emergencies, but I myself would disagree and say that is the entire purpose of having an emergency fund in your savings. My generation and students who are just entering high school probably feel like credit has been around forever, and even I talked about it in my Three C's of Sales topic in Chapter 5. Credit has only been around for about 50-60 years, with the first actual credit card being issued in 1959. Just because you aren't a financial expert, or good with numbers, doesn't mean that you should be ignorant about your finances. You are already probably having to take out student loans or dissolve other personal debt, why would you want to add another pathway to debt on top of the load you have.

The goal is not to stockpile payments upon payments of things, it is to fully pay things off, with cash if you can, and eradicate yourself from debt so that you can build and invest from there.

. . . .

LONE WOLF TIP #12
Investing

This is another subject that has spanned multiple novels and books that I implore you to research and read to truly grasp the holistic view of investing. Even though I am not a mega-millionaire investor like Warren Buffett, George Soros, or Carl Ichan, I know that a staple rule in the investing world is to "save to invest, not invest to save." I personally have a focused but diversified portfolio of stocks and mutual funds ranging from tech, real estate, and food & beverage, but that is not the first step to investing. A lot of people believe that if they just find the right companies or stocks to invest in, then they will be set, but they would be following an "invest to save" methodology. The first thing you want to do is build up your savings account first and then allocate a portion of your income to investing, after you have secured a large portion of it to your savings. Acorns and Stash are two apps that deal with buying and selling stocks and are very good for beginners that are new to investing. It is where I started out, buying fractional shares and putting in a little money at a time to get that experience under my belt. Robinhood is another app that is geared towards those who have a better understanding of the industry and the market, and is the next level, if you will, of investing compared to the former two.

. . . .

Real estate is also a method of investing that has a lot of buzz and hype around it. Real estate has brought people a multitude of financial gain...as well as a detrimental blow of financial losses. My parents own a rental property in the form of a condo, so I have had an inside look into what that process looks like. I have had to manage that property for my parents somewhat, which helped teach myself the ropes, and go through all of the repairs, tenant solicitation, paperwork forms, and everything else you can think of. Sometimes going through the fire is the best way to find out how to get burned, and also how to avoid those things next time.

When I continually mention savings and an emergency fund and all of those other things, I know it can be a bit confusing. It still is confusing to me at times, and I am still scratching the surface. However, what you should do with regards to building your savings, is open a new and separate savings account apart from the main account you use and use this as an emergency fund. This is a fund that replaces the use of a credit card for emergencies and allows you to borrow from yourself with no interest if your car breaks down, or there is a medical accident, or you are behind on your rent or tuition. I recommend placing at least $1000 in there to start and grow it to where it can comfortably hold 3-6 months' worth of your expenses. You are probably thinking, where am I going to get $1000 to put into a savings account? Well if you have money to spend every month partying, or buying new clothes, or eating out often, you can use this as a personal discipline test to invest in yourself and build an emergency fund.

After you audit your own account and checking to make sure that you are not spending more money than coming in, allocating money towards building your emergency fund, then you finally have reached the stage where we can input investing into the equation. I personally used to think that I could just put a bunch of my money in the stock market and that will take care of everything, and I was on the right path because I was "investing" and trying to follow the path of those who were successful. However, I was not allocating money towards my expenses and was just throwing my money away. I recommend staying away from heavily investing in companies and the stock market until you handle your student loans, paying off your house and car, and any other debt, because if not then you are stretching yourself very thin financially.

Personally, I will be able to be a tad bit more aggressive in my investing because I have been blessed with a great post-grad situation. By the time I walk across the stage and receive my diploma from Miami University I will have a leg up on life because of the work I am putting in now. I will have my car paid off, an actual house that my parents are going to hand down to me because they are moving to Florida, and either a full-time job with a Fortune 500 company or continue to follow in my entrepreneurial path with J.C., and to never enter the "Rat Race" as Robert Kiyosaki mentions.

The most powerful investors can invest at a very high level because they are debt free and have the ability to allocate a significant portion of their income towards investing. Also, you want to be very cautious of the stock market. In the words of the critically acclaimed author Mark Twain, *"October: This is one of the peculiarly dangerous months to speculate in stocks. The others are July, January, September, April, November, May, March, June, December, August and February."* The market is extremely volatile if you look at it from the short term. Investing is the complete opposite methodology I explained earlier when I discussed checking your personal spending account every day, because investing is for the long-term. When you look at the etymology of words that is why it is called investing, it is because it is synonymous with time over a long period. However, this method of investing ties in with **LONE WOLF TIP #8** about looking rich vs. actually being rich. Instead of buying Starbucks every day, or the latest shoe from Nike, how about you purchase some stock into these companies instead. Don't buy the latest iPhone that you have been brain-washed to purchase, through expert marketing and branding, for $1,000. Alternatively, deal with the model you have and invest in Apple stock. Then you can purchase what you want based off of the dividends of the company, which is an amount of money the company pays either quarterly or annual to its stockholders based upon its profit. Without even realizing it, you have just taken the first steps in understanding how to build a stream of passive income.

Passive income is the principle idea of money working for you. That almost sounds too good to be true doesn't it? We have been taught through the public education system that going to work for somebody, and working really hard, is the only way to earn a living and receive money. That is why 80% of full-time workers say that they live paycheck to paycheck. (CNBC). There are other ways to earn money that are legal, where you have the opportunity to work for yourself, and build a stream of income that works for you, instead of the other way around. Investing in stocks and real estate can be a form of a stream of income, but there are hundreds of ways to generate passive income in this digital age. It is a general rule of thumb that to enter the conversation of being a millionaire, the average millionaire has about seven streams of income. The reason that Jeff Bezos became the richest man in the world, is because he literally built a stream of income, Amazon, that capitalized on nothing more than the growth of internet users at a staggering 1000%. You don't have to run an entire business to generate passive income however, you could sell items online, license music, drive your car for Uber or Lyft, or even listing an extra room in your house or apartment for rent. Now I don't want you to get confused and say, "Aren't I still working for money if I am driving people around in my car for Uber?" The difference is that you are not being paid a standard, salary wage by someone, you are working for yourself and on your own terms. That is what passive income truly is, it is the bastion for financial freedom and the release of time constraints such as the standard 9-5 work shift.

Even when we talk about building income streams and generating passive income, you have to understand that building wealth is not a get-rich-quick scheme. It takes sacrifice, hard work, and dedication, just like anything else. It is a disciplined process of budgeting, living just at or slightly below your means to stop hemorrhaging money and compiling debt, and investing in yourself through a basic understanding of financial literacy. I didn't learn anything about taxes, income streams, how to manage my accounts and debt, or even how to save and invest in high school, but if you want to be successful you have to go out and find this knowledge. Use my **LONE WOLF TIPS** and seek out mentors who understand what you want to learn, and start pursuing knowledge at a higher rate than you engage on social media and sliding into people's DM's. You are your own person. You are not your parents, friends, or siblings, so you have to find out what is your own personalized wealth plan for success.

This process and planning starts with understanding what REAL money is. Through my consulting firm, I am able to talk to a lot of clients and potential clients who all have the next best app, business, restaurant, or program that will shock the nation, and all they need to be successful is a large infusion of cash. One of my potential clients literally said, if I had half a million dollars then we would be in business and my project would be successful, and the investors would receive a return projected in the millions. Obviously, there are a lot of factors that coincide with fundraising for clients, but the basic principle is that the majority of the population does not understand what real money looks like. $200,000 is the number it takes to get into the top

1% of income earners in the United States, according to ASEC Data. Keep that number in mind, because here is a list of a few of the top-paying jobs in America, and their respective median salaries, based according to Glassdoor.

Physician - $195,842
Pharmacy Manager - $146,412
Enterprise Architect - $115,944
Software Development Manager - $108,879
Nurse Practitioner - $106,962
Engineering Manager - $105,260

Think about how long it takes someone to become a certified doctor. 12 years of formative schooling. 4 years of undergrad. 4 years of medical school. And finally, 3-8 years of completing your residency, on top of all the graduation tests and licensing you have to acquire. At least 23+ years of schooling to become credited in a profession that is arguably at the zenith of society, a medical doctor, and you are barely breaking into the 1% club of income earners. This is by no means a slight on any type of profession on the previous list, and there are certainly company bonuses and salaries that raise these professions way above the median based upon different denominations of your medical study, but these are real numbers here. So, when people say that they want to be a millionaire, be really successful, and achieve all of their financial and monetary dreams, they need to first have a grasp on what financial reality really is.

All of this previous advice and an understanding of what real money looks like, is what has kept me on the right track and moving in an upward trajectory. People are not successful financially without implementing financial habits alongside their quotidian balance habits. You have to be in control of every dollar that enters and leaves your accounts because once you have complete control over your finances, you can really focus on putting that energy towards generating passive income streams. Understand that there will be ups and downs financially, as there always is with life, but knowing you are budgeting your money, growing your savings and emergency fund, and actively reading about financial literacy are ways to level out the rollercoaster of financial empowerment.

Don't let the "I Deserve It" or the "Treat Yourself" mindset overcome you to the point of financial ruin and disrupt your financial planning. We live in an era of entitlement, where people think that they are just given the path to success and don't have to work hard for anything. I've seen people not go to class, not do their work, go out and spend money on clothes and Chipotle, lay in bed all day, and have the nerve to say, "I deserve this extra pizza or ice cream for dinner." Definitely take a mental break every now and then and do have fun and splurge on yourself when you can and it is accounted for, but don't trick yourself into saying you deserve it all, based on unwarranted actions. Always remember that money isn't everything, but that doesn't mean push it to the side and let someone else worry about it. Be in control of your own life and your own finances, and you will be leagues and bounds above the general population, and on the course to bettering yourself!

Chapter Recap

KEY IDEAS

1. The key to staying out of debt, is staying ahead of it and dispelling the myths behind it. You don't NEED good credit to have a good life.

2. Don't be scared to check your bank accounts. If you are worried about how much money you have in there, you are probably spending too much.

3. Building multiple streams of income is how people insert themselves into the top 1% of income earners.

REFLECTION QUESTIONS

1. Think about all of the things you personally pay for. How much of it is paid by someone else or your parents? Slowly start to alleviate those expenses from others and place them upon yourself.

2. Are you a big party person or avid "outgoer"? Think about how much you spend on these events and if it is really worth it every week.

3. What is the profession you want to enter, or are currently in? Are you supplementing that salary with other income streams?

4. Has society bombarded you with the notion of having credit? How can you utilize credit to your advantage and stay out of debt?

LONE WOLF TIP #11: **Understand Your Money**

LONE WOLF TIP #12: **Investing**

CHAPTER 8

Insight & Foresight

Throughout this book I have given multiple examples and parables that shed some insight into my own personal story, and what I believe is success for my age. I try my hardest to abide by my own habits that I have shared with you. I work out for an intense 45 minutes at least five times a week and making sure that my physical activity level is also supplemented with playing basketball or volleyball when I can. I am an avid reader, thoroughly engrossing myself in the Wall Street Journal, other financial and self-help books, as well as occasionally refreshing up on my Harry Potter series. I wake up every morning and complete my morning pushups, make my bed to the best of my ability, and meditate on how I am going to devour and attack the day ahead of me. Even when school starts to get stressful or life seems to be hitting me all at once, I still allow time to have a creative outlet with myself and my music. I am constantly learning new songs on the piano, singing, and writing my own music. Finally, I utilize my organizational system of checklists to keep myself up to date with all of my latest assignments and clients that I talk to.

There has probably been multiple times during this book that you have thought "Man this kid really has his head on straight and has it all under control," but that is simply not the case. The reason that I am moving in a positive direction towards success is because I have understood fear, failure, and rejection multiple times. I was turned down from MIT, couldn't afford going to Georgetown, have had numerous clients not do business with me, have failed collegiate exams, and even felt like I wasn't worth anything at certain low points of my life. It is because I know what failure is that I know to embrace it and move forward from it. You don't have to have everything figured out in high school, college, and even those critical years outside of schooling. Don't put loads and loads of pressure on yourself because you will drive yourself crazy and slip into the dark areas of life.

I will give you a perfect example of what I mean. My very first accounting class, Introduction to Financial Accounting, was the one class that almost made me question my belonging at college and made me want to drop out of school. I had done really well on the first exam and thought that accounting was going to be easy, until I got my second exam score back and I had gotten a D- on it. I thought it was a mistake and the professor put my test through the wrong grading methods and scales, but it was undoubtedly mine. My grade dropped from an A to an extremely low C-, and I had never gotten a C as a class score ever in my life. I called my parents and told them that I could never do accounting, the business school was too hard, and I didn't belong at this school. This may seem like a slight exaggeration, but it happens to students all of the time, especially during freshman year. My parents told me to study harder and keep pushing because I was admitted to the school and they chose me for a reason, so I should fully understand that I belong at this school.

So I went to office hours, I found a really cute girl who had an A in the class and had her tutor me, I did practice problems on my own and even watched accounting help videos online in preparation for the final. I was ready, and you couldn't tell me I didn't know how to write ledgers and understand the difference between debits and credits. I walked into the exam session, sat down in the very front with my suit on, and prepared to take the exam. There were some questions I felt a little nervous about, but for the most part, I felt really confident about the exam, even high-fiving the girl who had helped me and tried to set up a date to celebrate and get some food. Come to find out she had a boyfriend who was in another accounting class, but that's beside the point. When I got the exam back, I had gotten a C+ on it.

I was rocked to my core and screamed and was really upset. I thought that if you worked really hard, then you would get the outcome you desired right? When I told my parents, they weirdly applauded my efforts and told me good job, which I felt like I didn't deserve at all, and I asked them why they weren't mad at me for finishing this class with an overall C+. They said bluntly, "We saw you putting in all of the extra effort and really trying your best, and at the end of the day that's all you can do. You got A's in all of your other classes, so understand where your strengths and weaknesses are." So, what I want you to take away from my story is that, part of this is because of the **LONE WOLF TIP** about having a solid support system to pick you up when you fall, but also that you should be proud of giving your max effort into something no matter what the outcome. I understood that this is what college was going to be like, what being academically challenged was going to look like, and I used this instance as a stepping stone for the rest of my collegiate career.

Also understand that when you're in college, nobody expects you to have your entire life planned out. Unless you came in knowing exactly what you wanted to be, and stuck with it, there is no way that you are going to enter college and leave college with the same thoughts and aspirations in your head. College prompts you to grow as a person, learn about new things in your environment, and examine the world through different lenses. I came into college hard set on studying law and politics, and then majoring in Economics, until finally I switched it to Finance, and who knows if that is the major I will graduate with.

Now this is not to say be all over the place and switch your major three weeks before graduation and commencement, but you are allowed to change what YOU want to study and do because this is YOUR life. You are attending college to find out what you, and only you, want to do because this is the foundation for your life, and nobody else's. If both of your parents are doctors or lawyers, and you want to study business, computers, engineering, photography, or anything else, go ahead because it is your decision. Obviously make sure that it a sustainable life path for you to live off of, but never let peer pressure, or parental pressure, sway how you live your life. Even if you are not attending college or want to study a trade right out of high school, make sure that whatever you do you are doing with a purpose. If you do not have a clear purpose, you will be swimming in a sea of self-inflicted agony and continuous doubt and monotony.

I touched on this earlier in the book, but I really need you to understand that SUCCESS is a term that is thrown around carelessly and has been taken out of context many a time. Success is a personal perception. It may be the big house with the heated car seats, or a stable home with a loving family in the middle-class. Success may be working hard all year and getting that 4.0 G.P.A. and making the Dean's List, or it may be pulling a grade up from an F to a C+ because you worked extremely hard in that subject and it yielded positive results.

There is no secret formula to success. In this day and age there are people all over Facebook, Instagram, and YouTube, saying that they have been mentored by millionaires and are living life to the fullest without any type of job, so "pay me money" and I will show you how I did it. Remember how we talked about how wealth is not a get-rich-quick scheme, because there will be a lot of people who prey on those who are ignorant in business and mentally weak. Nothing comes from wanting or wishing something to happen, you have to go out and grab success by the throat with your own hands. You have the ability to take every single second of the day to improve yourself. What are you going to do with those 86,400 seconds in a day to work towards your goals? I have shown you what real money looks like, and all of the tips in here are not meant to make you rich by themselves within a certain time period. This world of success is all about the grind, hard work, and dedication to whatever you are doing, and if you never look failure in its eyes, you will never value true success.

I live by a lot of mantras and sayings, but one of them is "If not you, then who?" You have to first be your own source of motivation, because if you don't believe in yourself from the beginning, then nobody will, and you will be trapped in an endless cycle of mental poverty. It is ok to be a Lone Wolf sometimes. Take yourself out on dates, converse with yourself, learn to love yourself, and soon you will be able to edge closer and closer to being invincible and building your impenetrable mental fortress.

Another mantra that I have to stress 100% is from my father, is to never do a "half-ass" job. I never knew if that meant to put my back into it and use my "full-ass" or what, but now I truly understand that it is the basis for everything I talk about in the Lone Wolf Method. When you do something, you do it to the best of your ability every single time. Every time I bring J.C. a new client that we consult with, it doesn't matter if they are young or old, rich or poor, well versed in business or new to the game. He conducts the same process every single time because to him it is also a habit. If I do everything the right way in my eyes, and never slack off despite who it is, then excellence becomes the standard for my work, and I never have to worry about inadequacies. I strive to work extremely hard in business and school to show those who look up to me that you don't have to be a rapper, or a professional athlete in order to make something of yourself.

I want to share my Goals Journal with you so you can see the future aspirations that I want to achieve, and also so I have a personal checklist of mine to keep me humble and realize I always have something to work towards.

Benjamin's Goal Journal

1. Graduate Miami University with a bachelors business degree
2. Eradicate all fear of singing and performing my music
3. Pay off all of my parent's debt and give them everything
4. Be the guiding light and role model to my brothers and others
5. Establish a scholarship at Fairfield High School
6. Grow my emergency fund and continue investing wisely
7. Keep writing books about different topics
8. Create enough streams of income to enter the 1% club

I hope this book has provided you some tools that you didn't have before and reinforced the ones you already knew and have implemented in your own life. This book was written for no other reason than to educate you on some basic financial literacy information, help provide tips that will hopefully become habits that better yourself and shift your mindset in a positive way. I am not writing this book to tout myself around as an acclaimed author or to increase my personal status, I am writing this book because I have been blessed with an exceptional family who has instilled in me faith, purpose, and discipline and I want to be able to share those lessons I have learned with everyone who wants to be great in their own capacity. It is not that hard to be great, but you have to be disciplined, focused, and win the battle of attrition by continuing to fight against it. The battle of attrition is a term used mainly in the military where one side of the participants wins by continually wearing down the other to the eventual point of defeat. You are one side of the battle, and life is the other side. Life will hurl sticks, rocks, student loans, failures, self-doubt, loss of friendships, death of loved ones, and physical handicaps, but it is your duty to yourself and to your purpose to keep going no matter what. In the words of Martin Luther King Jr. *"If you can't fly then run, if you can't run then walk, if you can't walk then crawl, but whatever you do you have to keep moving forward."*

Chapter Recap

KEY IDEAS

1. Failure is nothing more than a stepping stone to success.

2. You don't have to know exactly where you are going to school, what you will study, or what your profession will be. As long as you keep moving in the right direction, you will be fine.

3. Some people say that you can't predict the future, but I believe that setting goals is a way of having some say in writing your own future.

REFLECTION QUESTIONS

1. What are some times that you have tried your very best and still believed that you have "failed"?

2. What are some of the goals that you have set for your life? How committed are you to achieving these realities?

3. What are some of the things you have learned throughout and what was your favorite chapter and why?

4. How are you personally going to win against your own battle of attrition?

Lone Wolf Tips

About the Author

A graduate of Fairfield Senior High School, Benjamin Phillips III succeeded at the top of his class and was awarded with Summa Cum Laude awards upon graduation. Benjamin is a student at Miami University in Oxford, Ohio where he is enrolled in the nationally renowned Farmer School of Business. On campus, he is very involved with the Multicultural Business Association, the Governmental Relations Network, and is a steadfast voice for the current generation of students. He holds the highly coveted position of Student Assistant in the Dean's Suite, where he is the liaison between multiple Fortune 500 companies and the Farmer School of Business. He also has interned with prestigious accounting firms such as Ernst & Young, and is Junior Consultant at J.C. Baker & Associates, a global comprehensive consulting firm based in Cincinnati, Ohio. Benjamin is also an avid public speaker to students to prepare them for what lies ahead.

Benjamin is available to speak to your class, group, or church. For more information, email him at LoneWolfMentality1@gmail.com.